D0810650

# GRAIN *of* TRUTH

# GRAIN *of* TRUTH

## THE ANCIENT LESSONS OF CRAFT

# ROSS A. LAIRD

Walker & Company
New York

First published in the United States of America in 2001 by
Walker Publishing Company, Inc., by arrangement with
Macfarlane Walter & Ross, Toronto

Library of Congress Cataloging-in-Publication Data

Laird, Ross A.
Grain of truth : the ancient lessons of craft / Ross A. Laird.
        p.    cm.
Includes bibliographical references and index.
ISBN 0-8027-1389-0 (alk. paper)
    1. Woodwork.    2. Handicraft.    3. Wood.    I. Title.
TT180 .L25 2001
684'.08 — dc21        2001026346

Printed in the United States of America
2  4  6  8  10  9  7  5  3  1

To Elizabeth –

sage, trickster
keeper of long dreams
always my brightest talisman

# CONTENTS

# ACKNOWLEDGMENTS

My children, Avery and Rowan, have helped to forge and hold the crucible of this work. They sustain, along with many other family members and friends, the guiding flame of my life. To my father, who was my first guide in the work of hands, I owe a particular debt of gratitude.

I am indebted to Sherry Penn, Sharon Butala, Craig Mosher, Nancy Billias, Ann Ross, Carol Barrett, Don Shapiro, Dougal Fraser, Joanne Tonita, and Ronald Peter St. Coeur for their mentorship, insight, and camaraderie through what has been a rich and formidable journey.

John Macfarlane, Jan Walter, and Gary Ross, my editor at MW&R, took on this project with enthusiasm and trust. I am thankful for a door opened.

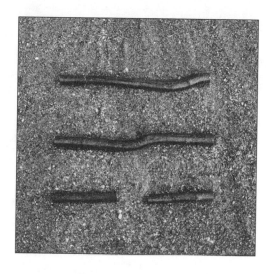

# W I N D

I STEP OFF THE GRAVEL PATH, HERE WHERE THE
shimmering summer air gives way to a darker quiet in
the forest. A woodpecker perches on a nearby cedar, its
rhythmic *tock* echoing clearly through the trees. Beyond
the threshold where ragged path meets forest floor, the
shaded ground is littered with dry branches of birch, fir,
and alder. Some are bright white, the bark still lustrous
and pristine. Others have lain here since spring and are

now mottled and dark, the wood beneath the skin graying as it reaches toward the soil.

This is a dangerous place. Each year a few of these birches rot away, fall toward the ground, and are hung up by companion trees. They lean precariously onto slim branches, easily dislodged by wind and rain and simple decay. I have recently removed such a deadfall, nudging it from its delicate position above the cabin and guiding it to where it fell within inches of the garden swing. Its shattered trunk still lies across the front lawn.

In this grove, tucked alongside the winding path and unhindered by human concerns, the trees grow recklessly, large and small tight together, the high canopy a mix of massive cottonwoods and tough, scrubby fir. The forest floor is knee-deep with sharp sticks, dry leaves, and hidden holes shaped by the unseen forces of this place. I move slowly in my bare feet, scanning the ground for branches about as thick as my index finger, newly fallen wood that I can use for handles on the cabinet I've built. They must be just right: long enough to offer six or eight inches of clear grain, neither too thick nor too straight. I wade farther out, back toward the rear fence that I can just make out, its posts blending into the surrounding landscape after thirty years of confident neglect. I gradually gather a collection of contenders as I go, meandering through the landscape, eyes softly focused. I want the forest to offer up the pieces, to point them out to me as gifts. I don't want to be a thief here.

After a quiet half hour I have twenty pieces tucked under my arm. I'm about ready to turn back when I come across a long, graceful branch of uniform thickness, larger than I can use yet beautifully curved and elegant. Its white bark is flecked with amber streaks, the signs of initial decay layering the surface with a variety of color and torture it had never known on the limb. The long fall from the body of the tree, the separation from unity, has given this branch, as it does so many things, a glow of intensity. Loss brings out its depth.

The shape of the branch, the way it sweeps smoothly along its length, suggests a myriad of uses in furniture building. I could simply cut it to length for one of my projects, leaving the bark intact as an unusual decorative element. In woodworking there's so much emphasis on refining the wood, making it clear and straight, hiding its diversity with finishes, that such a piece, unaltered and innocent, would be highly effective. I imagine a Windsor chair with a set of traditional spindles flanking a central rear column of unworked birch, its white and russet tones a fluid pillar.

I pick up the longer piece and bundle it with the rest, my small collection growing more unwieldy. As I move back toward the cabin in a wide arc across the forest floor,

I see other shapes, other forms in the fallen wood: the curve of a table rail, a knothole shaped like a whimsical recessed drawer pull, the twisted finials of imaginal bed-posts. This is where creative work starts for me — with openness, a sense of possibility, an invitation earned through quiet rambling, and a willingness to start with nothing. It doesn't often stay this way, but the beginning is always a kind of wonder.

I return to the rough lawn above the beach and lay the pieces out, looking for the best match for my cabinet handles. It's now late in the afternoon, and clouds above the distant western hills glow as the sun descends behind them. A band of deeper orange almost the color of ripe peaches spreads in a fringe across the lower reaches. The forest fire of two weeks ago has left a wake of ash in the air, drawing deep hues of rich, lambent color from the sky.

My two-year-old son, Avery, waddles up from his collection of sand toys and picks up one of the sticks I've collected, thwarting my efforts at neat organization. I want a row, a clean row of twenty pieces arranged by length and by character that I can winnow down to two or three finalists. Avery inspects the stick, looks for something in it to hold his attention, becomes indifferent almost immediately and tosses it behind him. I retrieve the discarded piece and reposition it, only to find he's dislodged another. We go around in this way for a few frustrating minutes. Eventually I convince him that holding on to one piece and sitting beside me on the lawn is a better alternative than banishment to the cabin.

There's wind on the lake now, a squall that kicks up tiny whitecaps. Not the whitecaps of the sea, their ragged momentum driving a head of foam six or ten or twenty feet across a swell deep enough to swallow a dinghy: what we used to call a choppy sea. No, these whitecaps are only a few inches high, a foot at best. Their quick, darting motions fizzle in the flattening wind. A squall like this can come and go in twenty minutes, though I've seen it gust strongly enough to bring down large cedars on the shore. Today the wind is only playing. By the time I got out there with the windsurfer, the breeze would be gone and I'd be left balancing on quiet water, waiting for a little gust, tugging the sail toward me in a slow rhythm trying to make my own air. It looks enticing out there, just enough wind, but I can sense that it's ephemeral, a ghost on the water, something to draw me in and leave me awash in my own enthusiasm.

I return my attention to the wood on the grass and begin to select those pieces that looked promising in the forest but now, under the stronger light of the shore, don't seem right. Too thin. Beginning to rot on the underside. Too many sharp branch ends. Too straight, like a machined dowel. Eventually I find two that seem ideal. Both are dry enough that the light bark flakes off easily, revealing clear yet varied grain beneath. They have a slight curvature, an undulation that runs through them almost like a wave, twisting them slightly along their length.

I clean off the residue of bark carefully from the surface of the wood. Then, taking one of my carving knives, the one with the *pau ferro* handle and a blade that reminds me of a raven's beak, I carefully slice through one of the pieces in two spots, leaving a trimmed length of about six inches. Measuring against the first piece, I select the most promising section of the second and cut it to a matching length. I now have the beginning of two handles: sinuous pulls that will gently arch out from the cabinet face and invite the hand.

I retrieve my portable drill from the cabin, banging the screen door on my way in and out, and drill two small holes about the diameter of a pencil partway through each handle. The holes are an inch or so in from each end and will house the pegs, or tenons, connecting the handles to the cabinet. Next I choose one of the smaller discard pieces, trim off four short sections and carve them to fit snugly into the handle holes, leaving protruding ends to fit matching holes in the cabinet face.

Carving of this kind, where small parts are involved, requires a specific posture and manner of holding the knife. I'm not whittling, slicing the blade away from my body as I used to do when I was a kid with my Swiss army knife before I lost it through a hole in the dock at Jericho Beach. That approach allows the blade to follow the direction of the wood's grain, digging too deep or skating and rattling off the surface. I'm using a different strategy here. I wrap my fingers gently but snugly around the handle of the knife; the blade extends beyond the edge of my index finger. My thumb is held firmly away from the blade, almost as though I were hitchhiking but with the thumb pointed toward my chest rather than upward. My palm faces down and my wrist is turned slightly outward. This hand position allows the blade to be drawn along the wood toward my body; my thumb and index finger rest on the surface and move together, the distance between them constant. Before I learned to carve in the manner I now prefer, what woodworkers call a chip-carving approach, I would fix my thumb in place on the wood and use it as a lever to draw the blade toward me, trying to stop the cut before it reached my thumb but seduced by the fact that I achieved maximum leverage as the blade approached my skin. I have scars on the thumb of my left hand as souvenirs of that potato-peeling approach. Today I use my arm and shoulder as a lever to pull the blade firmly and exactly through the wood, using my hand as a natural jig to hold the tool.[1] My knife is at least as sharp as a razor and I am able to shave off the wood in clean, precise increments. It takes only a few minutes, paring and then checking the fit of a piece in its intended hole — its mortise — to shape all the pieces so they fit fully together with moderate pressure.

I inspect all the pieces once again, looking for anything I've missed. I trim a couple of rough spots where
tiny buds had once grown through the pores of the wood.
When everything seems ready, I place a dab of glue in
the handle holes and gently tap the tenons home. It's a
snug fit. Even without glue the joints would be tight, but
this is newly fallen wood I'm working with, green wood,
and it will contract slightly as moisture is drawn out of it
by the warmer air in the cabin. In six months the tenons
will have lost a few thousandths of an inch in diameter,
enough for a quick tug to loosen them in their mortises.
The glue is necessary to lock them in place, to fill all the
spaces inside the joint.

I'm always panicky with glue. I routinely apply too
much, and excess oozes out of the joints. I can never quite
convince myself that a little goes a long way, even with the
expanding super-strength glue I use. I worry, imagining
I'll starve the joint by making insufficient contact with the
glue across the surface area of the wood. I suspect my
worrying is unnecessary, indulgent, irrational. Yet I spend
many familiar hours cleaning up dried glue on most of
my projects. Sometimes I apply wax to the sections I don't
want the oozing glue to penetrate. This helps quite a bit,
but getting the wax off can be a chore, too; as with the
glue, I usually slather it on with excessive enthusiasm.

I manage to be confident about the fit of these
joints and resist the temptation to apply more glue than

necessary. After a few minutes, when the glue has begun to expand inside the pieces, I notice with gratitude that none is spilling out. At least I won't have to clean up glue today.

The distant clouds shine with indigo and light the landscape with an amethyst hue. I can see clearly my favorite patch of open green near the summit of a far-off hill. I gaze up there quite a bit on summer days, wondering what's on that hill. It could be a clear cut, a farm, a pasture. But I've always imagined it to be a secret field of possibility, a pristine and inviting territory where I might find all the vanished creatures of the earth. It seems so distant, an emerald glistening far up the slope of a verdant landscape. Yet at times I can almost make out shapes moving up there: peacocks and monkeys and Bengal tigers, white owls and speckled deer and something else I can't quite see. A chimera, a dancing fire, light playing in the darkness. Perhaps it's a dragon. The wind often blows from that direction.

I pick up Avery, my drill, and the two completed handles and head inside. The cabinet that waits to receive the handles is actually a large, floor-mounted cupboard. Elizabeth has been calling it a broom closet. I object to this on the principle that it offends my sensibilities as a craftsman. I am not a handyman, I tell her. I am not interested in the fact that the cabinet is in the shape of a small closet and has been designed to hold brooms. I'd rather be stubborn and preserve my imagined dignity than give in to the obvious.

The cabinet stands in the kitchen where the refrigerator used to be, filling the gap left when renovations required we move the refrigerator across the room. It has been painted the same loden green as the rest of the kitchen cabinets, some of which I made. Others were built thirty years ago by friends of Elizabeth's family, craftsmen who came out here from Kamloops on weekends, in the spirit of friendly reciprocity, and using only hand tools constructed the entire building. It's not an ambitious building, just a few hundred square feet of cinder block, tongue-and-groove fir paneling, and a roof buttressed by modest beams. Yet the collaborative endeavor of those many friends in this quiet place reflects a community sentiment and family connection that one rarely sees anymore.

Elizabeth and I joke that a true friend is someone you'd ask to help you move. Those craftsmen, first-generation immigrants from Italy, spent countless hours out here working, laughing, taking the time to build a welcoming cabin with a central, massive, magnificent brick fireplace. In that fireplace we can build bonfires the size of those we see other people making on the beach. Who among us in the city has such friends?

I never knew most of the people who populate the first stories of this place. Yet I feel intimately connected to them when I come across faded pencil marks on top of a beam or feel my way through the wiring system, sensing why a junction box is here, not farther along where it seems it should be but right here, above where the space heater was supposed to go but was never installed. There are stories about the windows, how difficult they were to install, and about how Elizabeth's grandfather worked with the cinder blocks. I find small clues to these stories as I work, stumbling upon oddities or faint signs of another's hand.

A familiar mood of belonging, of place, sweeps forward from what has gone before and moves through me, holding me within its wide grasp. I continue the work of connection and community that was started before me, guided by the invisible hands of those who first made this place a haven of lasting beauty and solace. I have been drawn gently but irrevocably into their circle, and by continuing the modest vision laid down with the first shale walkway tiles I acknowledge them as among my truest ancestors.

I carefully drill two sets of holes in the cabinet doors to hold the handles. I do this by eye, without measuring to see if they're exactly aligned. I tell myself my skills are so refined that I have no use for levels and tape measures, but the truth is that I'm excited to see the handles in place and my toolbox is inconveniently across the room. After applying just a little bit of glue to the holes – it seems like too little – I push the handles into their mortises, locking them into place. I pause, relaxing with the satisfaction of a completed job, even a small job like this, which keeps me tensely alert until I'm done.

I step back for a final look. No gaps or twists are visible in any of the joints. Now Elizabeth comes over for her ritual inspection. This always worries me; her inspections are a true test of a project. She often sees things I've missed, and it's no surprise when she comments that one handle is slightly lower than the other. Looking closely, I can see the imbalance as well, but the gentle curve and irregularity of the handles makes the misalignment subtle; it could have been intentional. I offer my traditional response to my oversights and blunders: "It's a design element." "Yes," she says, "I was sure that's what it was."

I began coming to this place fourteen years ago, when I first met Elizabeth. We spent a week in late August playing backgammon on the beach and watching hawks in the nearby trees. In those days the cabin had fallen into neglect: ants had burrowed holes through the roof and the smell of damp pervaded the rooms. The mesh on the screen door failed to keep the mosquitoes out. There were still plums in the garden, and even though the stream that once ran along the edge of the property had long since dried up and moose no longer followed it down to the shore in the early mornings, their great antlers dipping in the cool waters as they drank, the place retained its wonder.

During those first few years we cleaned things up, organizing and tidying and trying to find which of the air mattresses was still serviceable. As time went on we began to tackle more ambitious projects: painting, new floor coverings, a kitchen renovation. Each year we'd spend the bulk of our two-or-three-week holiday fixing, modifying, repairing. We've done quite a bit by now, and as the next generation of children begins to find resonance with this place, its renewal seems like a fine endeavor indeed. The work has been an initiation for me, a sustained immersion in the life of a family that I slowly grew to know, an awakening into lasting relationship and an invocation of my desire for a richer life, an invocation that at times I was utterly unaware I was making. My work here, my faithful absorption in the tasks of rebuilding a place of respite, has led me into the heart of Elizabeth's family and has ushered me, not always gently, toward a larger sense of what it means to be awake, to be alive.

From where I'm standing beside the newly finished cabinet I can see out the front window, the one that still has masking tape around the sill where Elizabeth's sister began, but didn't complete, a new coat of paint. The tape is stuck firmly now, its adhesive cured by months of exposure to the warm air. Someone will have to get in there with a razor knife – that task and countless others are on the long list we keep on the fireplace mantel. The whitecaps are still out there, their dark bellies and white foam heads like small dragons undulating across the water. I think of Ogopogo, the great serpent that is said to haunt the deep waters of the lake over the hills from where we are. Towels on the clothesline strung between two trees out front are beginning to loosen as the wind whips them, their designs like emblematic prayer flags repeatedly curled and then flattened, the wind speaking its own sign language.

This property lies just over an hour's drive east and north of Kamloops, British Columbia. It's situated near the end of the paved road, in the crescent of a wide bay where Canada geese pause each autumn to collect themselves for the long journey south. Ten minutes down the road the pavement gives way to oiled gravel that wends forty miles farther into territory rising in a series of steppes toward the foothills of the Rocky Mountains. The air here possesses a clear ring, as though a distant bell has been struck and now trembles softly, just beyond the threshold of hearing.

We often ride our bikes up the road past green fields to where a shallow stream washes over stones caressed smooth by time, their surfaces diverse with the music of color. Black stones, jet black, collect in pools along the shore. Azure and emerald veins run like sinew through boulders on the streambed. Countless glittering eyes of granite stare out from dark niches with implacable clarity. Sometimes we find tiny pink stones, as though a nomadic coral has accompanied the salmon who come to spawn, and has preserved the death hue of that indomitable fish in its own deathless heart.

I've always wondered where the stream leads as it wanders back into the country of the unseen. I imagine the colors we find in the stones merging together at a source deep in the mountain, the waters reaching toward the formless where wind also begins. Toward what the ancient Taoist sages called Wu Chi, the primordial creative genesis of all things. Those sages lived in places like this, doing simple physical work, dedicating themselves to the elemental creative force of Tao, whose message they heard on the wind. Taoist philosophy is imbued with countless tales of them: holy men and prophets and healers of the most profound and simple character. The breadth of their wisdom is astounding, from medicine and geomancy to poetry and cosmology. Their tradition still shapes, after 5,000 years, much of Asian culture. The archetypal trigrams, images that represent the timeless shapes of life energy, are their creation.

Those ancestral teachers, shrouded in mystery and separated from us by an abyss of time, frequented specific sites of sacred contemplation – mountain abodes or valley shrines – where they anchored their esoteric pursuits in the rituals of daily life. It was always from a secure foundation that they leapt into the unknown. Thus, in a discourse on working with the initiatory energy of wind, the Taoist *I Ching* confirms "it is beneficial to have some-where to go."[2] A place of solace and refuge. A ground that nurtures, that offers a larger purpose, the way the forest offered the cabinet handles.

The wind moves upon the water, leading me outside to where the ropes of the hammock have started to loosen from the bole of a broad cedar. The swish of twisted strands in the wind shows me where to tie the new knot. The warmth of evening drifts toward the cabin as the breeze meanders through cottonwoods on the shore. The day slows. By nightfall stillness will take possession of this place. Even so, a trunk will creak, wavelets will ripple onto the shore, leaves shimmering in the dark will hum a melody just beyond catching. In the grove out back, the slanting sun shoots dark, amber rays across the white trunks of birch trees. A leaf skitters briefly across the slate tiles of the patio, comes to rest, slides scratchily again, pauses, then resumes its slow dance toward the beach.

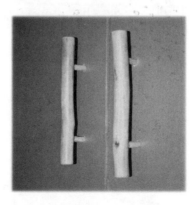

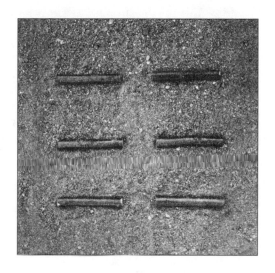

## 2

# E A R T H

THE TIPS OF MY FINGERS ARE GRIMY AND BLACK,
like a coal miner's. Dark, umber streaks trace their way up
my index and middle fingers, smudging into the pores of
my skin, outlining the bloody scratch where the blade
slipped off the sharpening stone. The area surrounding the
nail of my right index finger is sore, the skin stretched from
too much pressure, back and forth, back and forth over
the stone. I've put a fabric bandage, the tough industrial
kind, over the tip of my finger as a buffer. It, too, is black

and wet, dyed by the swarf washed loose from sharpening. The index and middle fingers of both hands form a horizontal V over the top of the blade, right under left, the weight of my arms and shoulders pushing down on the stone as the blade glides forward. I begin each stroke at the top edge of the stone, holding the blade securely at an angle of thirty degrees, steadying my arms, drawing a breath. Then I push down, hard, and guide the blade onto the stone, clear along its length, lifting it up at the end and easing the pressure. As it moves, the blade makes a sound like tiny pebbles washing up on a wayworn beach.

The rhythm of the work is precise and demanding. There must be sufficient pressure on the stone to remove metal from the blade, but too much force can skew the blade's smooth path. Moreover, the surface of the stone must be kept absolutely level. This is accomplished by covering its entire surface in the sharpening process, going over the center as well as the edges. Repeatedly following the same path with the blade wears down the center of the stone and creates a shallow valley that curves the blade while sharpening it. This is sometimes useful for specialized work but is generally a frustrating nuisance. And this steel: it's not the soft stuff that goes into factory-made planes from the hardware store – this is far harder, more susceptible to corrosion but tougher by what feels like orders of magnitude. I can sharpen a new production blade to high tolerances in about ten minutes; I've been at this for at least half an hour, my back aches from the exertion, and only now am I seeing the bright signal of polished steel appear near the edge of the bevel. The bevel of a blade, not the cutting edge itself but the ramp that leads up to the edge, must be smooth and flat enough that you can clearly make out your reflection in it – no indolent muddiness. That's what I'm going for here.

I apply considerable compressive force against the fresh steel, pushing it onto a Japanese water stone hundreds of times in a rhythmic motion that has me puffing and sweating. Bits of the stone are coming loose, sloughed off by the blade's hardness, mixing with water and tiny particles of steel to make the dark mess covering my fingers. The stone is supposed to wear away like this, the used-up grains breaking off and exposing new and sharper grit. But this seems excessive: the stone is being diminished layer by layer, the equivalent of many regular sharpenings, while the steel slowly, like a glacier casually carving through a mountain, takes shape.

I'm getting tired. Rowan, my five-year-old daughter, keeps calling me to come inside and get her some juice. I tell her it will be just another minute or two. Four times I've said that, and I don't like doing it. I don't want to be a dad who never follows through. And I'm not. But the damn steel is so stubborn, so implacable – it wants to wear me out, wants me to prove that I have the strength to meet it, to hold it, to use it. At least that's what it feels like. There's a battle going on, a fight for control of the power inside this gleaming shard of tempered iron. When I hold it up to the light, it shines like a fragment of a star, a jewel brought out into the light after long darkness.

One last rush, a final push through twenty or thirty hard strokes on the stone, checking and rechecking the edge where the two angles of the steel meet. I want the bevel and the back to come together crisply and precisely so that the fierce edge leaves no room for light to make a reflection. I want my eye to follow the quicksilver brightness of the blade down to where it disappears, its light abruptly ending at the moment of greatest refinement. Absence of light is what marks an edge as truly sharp; a blade that shines at its edge is dull. The perfect blade is invisible.

Such philosophical considerations make the act of sharpening more than what it would otherwise be: a long, tedious process of wrestling with materials that resist me at every turn, hard physical exertion punctuated by moments of sharp pain as the blade sinks into my skin after a second of inattention. And though the blood washes out, dark stains from the swarf do not. It takes several days for new skin, soft and destined for hardship, to emerge out of the cracked landscape of the old. Yet of all the rituals of working with wood, all the diversity and challenge of it, sharpening is among the most meditative acts. The most physical and the most ethereal. It's not a

clean meditation, not refined or rarefied or purely ecstatic
– no, it is a meditation of the earth, of sweat and blood
and dark stone. Sharpening sluices away thoughts of being
elsewhere, of being greater or lesser, of calculated plans
and secret schemes, of expansive future and protected
past, of hunger in all its forms, of specialness and wisdom
and imagined clarity. Sharpening slices through the illusion that being human is something greater than the earth
itself. It presents the simple truth of the body, stained
hands and useless protests creating a tiny shard of noth-
ingness. Sharpening makes everything disappear into that
invisible edge.

This ragged wrestling between the steel and my stub-
bornness is a negotiation. The steel asserts its own dignity,
its insistence that I treat it with the reverence it deserves.
I must never forget that anything we accomplish together
is a collaboration. And I assert my own strength, my demand
that the steel allow itself to be guided by my vision of
what is *true* – right angles and level surfaces but also the
more elusive truths this work presents. In this collaboration I must eventually surrender to that which takes shape
between the tools and myself, or stop altogether. I am
building and refining relationships with the tools, they are
spirits in a real way, and no amount of personal inflation
or enthusiasm can diminish the fact that they enable the
work to flourish. I am their guide, perhaps, their steward,
but tools make the wood come alive.

Two more strokes. One more. My arms ache. As the final stroke glides off the edge of the stone, I turn the motion into an upward swing and bring the steel into the light. I lean forward to check my work. I can't see any scratches on the bevel or the back. My reflection is clear. The wedge tip of the blade shines almost to the leading edge, where it abruptly grows dark, inscrutable.

I come in from the shop and pour a glass of apple juice for Rowan. She's reading a kids' magazine at the kitchen table and calls me over to look at pictures of a Komodo dragon wreathed in volcanic steam. She asks me if there are still other kinds of dragons, fairy-tale dragons, on the earth. I think of the field of green that is visible from the lake, the place of all vanished creatures and fantastic beings yet to be born.

At the kitchen table, looking out onto one of Vancouver's first crisp days of autumn and feeling myself observed by the slitted eyes of the Komodo dragon on the page, I consider the project before me. I am making a small and simple box, a vessel to hold the ashes of Elizabeth's grandmother. I am embarking on a journey of reverence for a soul traveling into the invisible. This is why I need my blades to be sharp, my tools as true as I can get them. When the box is completed it will be placed within the earth, eventually to be reclaimed with the treasure it contains. The box is an offering to the earth, and because of this I need my work to be honest, purposeful, compassionate. I must not forget my own source.

Back in the shop I lay the wood pieces on my worktable: six boards of different sizes, all Brazilian purpleheart, a hardwood noted for its toughness on tools but deep finished luster when worked properly. This wood has no need of varnishes or stains; simply polishing the surface with a small amount of beeswax yields a deep glow, the distinctive indigo silk of prayer flags fluttering in a smoky wind.

I clamp one of the pieces in the vise, long edge up, and run my plane with its new blade across the surface. Small purple twists of shavings glide to the floor. I run my blackened finger along the edge, checking for bumps or ridges that would indicate a problem with the plane. Everything seems fine, at least with the tools and materials. But I'm nervous. This is no coffee table or bunk bed; it is a sacred object. This makes me more cautious, less certain, aware at every step of a peculiar feeling that pervades the shop. I must not be cavalier, or impatient, or allow myself to fall into the many traps I set for myself in the work. This box, which will carry Sadie's ashes across an unfathomable threshold, must be worthy of its task. And so I must be worthy of mine. Sadie would laugh at this high-minded tone. She would want something utilitarian: no fuss, no extra effort. That's the way she was.

With this in mind, and with the Komodo dragon still peering at me from inside my head, I begin.

I spend an hour at the tablesaw, first checking the intended size of the six pieces – top, bottom, and four sides of the box – then cutting to final dimensions. I've decided to use mitered joints for the sides and bottom as this will allow the corners to meet precisely at their edges and create the effect of the grain wrapping itself around the box. I make sure the sides are cut from a single board and number them with bits of masking tape so they can be fitted in sequence.

Cutting miters is a tricky business if, like me, you routinely make errors in measurement. The blade of the saw seems always to be angled too far over, I can never remember which way the miter is supposed to go, I can't decide whether to cut from the left or the right, toward or away from the angle of the blade. I make close to a dozen test cuts in scrap stock and mark every piece of purpleheart with a length of tape that says "inside," so I know which side faces up on the saw. Each tape segment also has a diagram of which way the cut should slope and two arrows that point to the mitered edges. This is more information than I need, but I've made too many baseboards half an inch short by cutting the miter in the wrong direction. I need a fail-safe strategy.

Making an enclosed box is straightforward in some ways; only six pieces, and the joinery is uncomplicated.

Yet a well-made box is not easy to construct. The small number of pieces means higher tolerances are required. Fewer joints means more stress on each joint. The miters must fit together with no slop at all and be absolutely square. Otherwise the entire box will be misaligned as inaccuracies accumulate from one corner to the next. Nowhere in woodworking is accuracy more fundamental than in box-making. Here then, at the beginning, I must make all the parts straight and true. This process requires of me the same qualities that I am trying to coax from the wood.

Sawing the miters is accomplished without incident but with much anxiety. I pause after each cut, wondering if I've inadvertently put the tape on the wrong side, inventing things that could go wrong. What if the lights suddenly go out? What if I have low blood sugar and fall over onto the blade? What if I looked at the wrong side of the ruler when I measured, and transcribed the wrong cut marks? (This happens frequently, so as a possible catastrophe it's not too inventive.) Whenever I must use the tablesaw, these kinds of fears boil up inside me.

A tablesaw is a frightening machine. It is wondrously fast, accurate, and powerful, but it is also a demon. It can seize a piece of wood in its teeth and hurl it back at me, a missile of purpleheart or soft cedar or finely grained maple transformed from an object of beauty into a lethal projectile traveling faster than the top speed of my car. I have two ragged scratches in my shop from such incidents: one on the front wall, the other on the garage door. Both mishaps occurred during my first year in this craft, when I thought I was smarter than the spinning blade.

Certain procedures on the tablesaw are noted for their danger, for their likelihood of *kickback*. Few craftsmen, and fewer hobbyists, follow the recommended safety procedures. Not too long ago I saw a neighbor out in his driveway with his small tablesaw up on a couple of sawhorses: no shirt, no safety glasses, no hearing protection. He was sending through small cedar boards for his backyard fence, crosscutting them to size, making repetitive cuts, not watching what he was doing. The method he was using to feed the wood, with the material inadequately secured as it passed through the blade, allows the wood to twist toward the blade, where it can be suddenly drawn into the throat (as the opening for a blade is ominously termed), gobbled up, and spit out with whatever fingers happen to be holding the wood at the time. Crosscutting unsafely on a tablesaw is the best way to ensure you'll never use chopsticks again.

My neighbor was lucky; he kept his fingers. But the disturbing trend in woodworking is toward diminished anatomy as one's experience in the craft increases. I want, rather strongly, to avoid that fate. Thus I am hypervigilant when using the tablesaw, careful that the finicky blade guard – the first thing the typical owner of a new tablesaw removes – is firmly in place. I stand to the side of the blade to avoid surprising projectiles, make sure no one else is in the shop, wear short sleeves so nothing can get caught in the machinery, muffle the sound with extra-insulated hearing protectors, wear special high-impact safety glasses, and sweep the floor so there's nothing I can trip on. I slide the wood into the blade as though I were feeding a crocodile. For many woodworkers a peculiar, contrary attitude prevails: a machismo, a willful reckless-ness. Personally, I am quite receptive to the reality that any number of things in this work could kill me. The tablesaw is an angel of death. I try to respect that.

The whine of the tablesaw, which I imagine is the screeching and lamenting of all unready souls captured by its whining teeth, slows after the last cut and finally halts, the blade's claim on my fingers deferred yet again. I begin to relax.

Now the real work starts, the work of hands in simple moments, of quiet and attention and the rhythm of time. Although I appreciate the raw muscle and speed of power tools, I'm ambivalent about them. They are indifferent to the quality of my work, cutting without regard for the beauty and diversity of the materials. Hand tools, con-versely, will purr and cough and shout. They change with the way I work, adapt themselves to the materials, remind me of their music at every turn. Pick up a well-used and loved plane, one with a history of being cared for, and see how it skates incisively across the grain even when the blade is dull. Listen to the distinctive whisper it makes as shavings spiral smoothly from its throat. Those shavings are the individual notes a plane makes in its song.

Try to shave down anything at all, even soft redwood, with a plane that is either new from the factory or has lain in neglect. Immediately the blade jams in the wood, tearing out chunks of the grain, rattling on the surface, making the sound of boots crunching on wet gravel as small shavings grind unevenly out. It is one of the unspoken truths of woodworking that tools speak to the craftsman; they respond to a gentle and caring touch.

If I am receptive enough, working with hand tools is always a discovery. The tools point to new ways of doing things, new possibilities for drawing out the invisible and refined energy of the work. The ancient Taoist sages spoke of opening to mystery, opening through stillness, as the first act of understanding. Working with hand tools teaches, in a pragmatic way, the art of stillness. Tools teach this so well because they come from the earth, from stone and wood and fire. They have not forgotten the language of that source.

The symbol that begins this chapter, the Taoist trigram for Earth, contains an open column of emptiness between two sets of lines. The common way to think about this image is to view it as three broken lines, three lines with a gap. But then the focus is on the lines and not the white space. The important element is the column of emptiness; it denotes the potential of energy to flow through. This requires a purposeful surrender, a willingness to be taught by tools or the wind or a horse leaping a fence. As the Taoists say, "Taking the lead, one goes astray; following, one finds the master."

The tablesaw yields a cut that requires final trimming with a plane, so I arrange the boards on my worktable and inspect the cut surfaces. Then I place the pieces one at a time in the vise, and taking care to keep the sole of the plane absolutely flat on the surface of the cut—I don't want to round over the edge or trim the miter out of true—I slowly pare away the pattern of small ridges left by the saw's carbide teeth. Almost no effort is required, no cajoling or forcing. Small indigo strands flutter through the throat of the plane.

There are twelve mitered faces to trim: the four sides of the box each have two, and the bottom has four. When I'm done, I test-fit the pieces, wrapping long elastic bands around the four sides. The grain match around the corners is excellent. The bottom fits nicely in the angled niche created for it by the surrounding sides. The overall effect of the wood is rich and warm but without ostentation. It's the kind of thing Sadie would have liked.

The assembled pieces take up about one square foot on the benchtop. I retrieve the single uncut board that will become the lid and carefully slide it over the assembly, watching that the joints do not shift out of alignment. I trace around the perimeter of the box, making the pencil lines clearly visible on the lid. Then I return to the table-saw and cut the remaining piece to size, leaving a small amount of excess to trim off during the final fit.

I'm not working from a plan here, or even from something I've seen. I'm designing as I go, improvising. Sometimes this approach can be wasteful, especially when I get halfway down a particular path and then realize I'm doing things in a way that doesn't seem right. But this project is simple enough, despite its faces and grooves and angles, that I can envision the entire process without needing to map it out on paper. Part of the appeal of this strategy is that it leaves me the opportunity to modify things, adapt the piece to its own natural way of being as I work. Once a plan is on the page I find it difficult to change things. When I let the process stay fluid, sketchily mapped out inside myself, my experience in the construction often leads to unexpected and rewarding changes.

When I have the main pieces together, tentatively unified by the elastic bands, I can see that my original idea for the design of the top would be heavy and ponderous, something the person it is designed for was not. The box requires a lightness, a sense of open solidity: present but not imposing. I decide to make an enclosed tongue-and-groove assembly that will allow the top to slide in from the front of the box. This requires a set of grooves, or dadoes, on three of the sides to act as a sliding mechanism for the top. The fourth side, the front of the box, must be trimmed down so the top can slide over it. And a tongue on the sides of the top must be shaped as well: all told, a dozen more cuts on the saw.

I take risks working in this way, designing in stages, always subject to arising problems that might have been avoided two or three steps back. But in planning out all the details I lose the possibility of discovery, the sense of adventurous not-knowing. Receptivity is sacrificed for certainty. Without a spirit of discovery, the work is just a technical exercise.

Many things have been lost in this craft, sometimes lost ages ago, things I might be rediscovering as I practice my own work. Imagine: the ancient Egyptians devised monuments and artifacts and sacred objects so refined that we cannot reproduce some of them today. In my little workshop garage I might rediscover the secret of crafts-men who, almost 5,000 years ago, made tall stone vases with long, narrow necks and wide, rounded bases. It's difficult to see how this was done; the Egyptians had no tools (as far as we know) capable of drilling and carving such interior shapes. Many of the hollowed-out bases were shaped to match the outside contours to such fine tolerances that the material is translucent. They did not leave tool marks to assist us in deciphering the mystery.

We could not reproduce those vases today; we do not possess tools of sufficient mastery to pass through a long, narrow stone neck and then, from the inside, carve out a wide base to match an exterior shape. Contemporary lathes equipped with special jigs can do similar work, but only on small pieces, and with much less accuracy than the Egyptians routinely achieved.

Many times in the work of craft I must devise a means of accomplishing tasks that seem unreasonably difficult, painfully labor-intensive, or downright impossible. Inventiveness, craftiness, is part of the process. Somehow the ancient Egyptians refined their creative instinct in such a way that marvels became commonplace. They discovered a great deal, some of which we are still deciphering. We do not know how, and to what purpose, they created the most architecturally demanding structures in the world, the pyramids at Giza. The range of theories about how it was done is impressive because the feat itself is so baffling. We could hardly lift the stones today, let alone set them in place. And the absence of steel – I have to remind myself of this, it seems so incredibly audacious, like forging a vast rainbow with sand.

There's magic in these works. Yet they were devised by simple craftsmen devoted to their trade, reaching to the furthest edge of their ingenuity, snatching the improbable from the jaws of the impossible. The magic is a human magic. Every craftsman, whether in wood or stone or words, strives in the shadow of hidden possibilities, searching for a means of making the mystery visible. What happens in my shop is no exception, though sometimes I must sit in silence for a long while, waiting for the answer to come, opening to the descent of the unfathomable.

Once the various grooves are cut to accommodate the top, and the tongue has been shaped to a tolerance slightly larger than its final dimensions (I will pare it down for a smooth fit later), the box is ready to be glued together. This is a simple procedure, as the mitered surfaces are unhindered by traditional splines, small wood segments inserted perpendicular to the angle of joints to increase their solidity. Modern high-strength glues make most splines unnecessary, though they are still used by many craftsmen for common procedures such as joining the boards of a tabletop. The boards will hold together just as securely without the splines, even past the breaking strength of the surrounding wood if the joint is finely made, but the tradition prevails. Old ways of working have remarkable persistence.

I make sure all the pieces are sanded smooth and ready for assembly. Then I wax the parts of the interior that lie alongside the joints; this way, even if there is some spillover, the glue will cure on the wax surface and not seep into the pores of the wood. The residue can then be sliced cleanly from the wood and the wax washed off with alcohol. Many such details accompany any glue-up:

fiddling with clamps, dry-fitting the parts, managing the order of assembly. These automatic routines free my attention and allow me to think about Sadie, to remember why, and for whom, I am engaged in this work.

Of the many stories and vignettes and remembrances of Sadie, I am consistently drawn to just one image: she's at the lake, on the concrete path, bent over her cane and intently, fiercely, squashing ants with its rubber tip. Sadie did not like ants. She was not a violent person by nature, but when it came to ants, with their implacable drive to infest the cabin, she was ruthless. Slowly, so much more slowly than the ants that she must have missed all but the most feeble adversaries, Sadie would grasp the scythe-like curve of the cane's handle, sight down the foreboding black shaft of her weapon, and strike with a sudden fervor, planting the end firmly, as firmly as one can press with a shock-absorbing tip, on her surprised foe. She'd pause, sometimes grinding the rubber in to catch any ants that might have hidden in pebbled crevices, then lift up for another shot. On it would go, a few minutes out of each day, this avenging angel in the shape of an old lady come to wrest from the encroaching hordes a sense of property and boundary.

I suppose the reason this story stays with me has something to do with its incongruity. Sadie was the archetypal grandma: sewing quilts and knitting afghans, baking cookies, always providing for her grandkids a safe haven.

Someone from an earlier time, the kind of person our society has increasingly turned its back on. Old, simple values. When she became unable to care for herself, she lived with Elizabeth's family; later, when her needs grew and no one in the family possessed the skills to care for her properly, she moved to an extended-care residence. She was visited there virtually every day by someone in the family. It took some effort to reconcile my knowledge of the deep, continuing connection and intimacy in Sadie's life with the sight of more than a hundred people gathered quietly in the massive common room at the residence, watching television, suffering from various degrees of being forgotten.

The joints glue together without any trouble. I remove a single small bead of cured adhesive on an inside corner with a light twist of the chisel. Now the top, which will require careful fitting. When finished, the box will be opened only once, to place Sadie's ashes inside, and then closed again forever. Any insistence on precision here is likely excessive, but for me the box cover has a metaphoric meaning: it represents the Gate of Life in Chinese medicine and alchemy, the Ming Men. That gate should open and close smoothly, without obstruction, squeaks, or scratches.

As I work on the sliding mechanism, paring the pieces carefully down by a few thousandths of an inch and test-fitting, paring again and testing again, I become aware that this project is slowing as I reach its final stages. This matches my usual rhythm in the work: mad rushing at the beginning, stolid persistence in the middle, relaxed quiet near the end, when the difficult tasks are completed and the weight of challenge lifts. Sometimes I worry so much at the beginning and in the middle – many things can go wrong – that I lose the joy of the work. That's when I stop, if I remember, and stay out of the shop for a few days. I'm almost always at ease near the end, when I know how much more time the project needs, when the likelihood of being surprised by something difficult diminishes, when whomever I'm making the piece for visits the shop and starts to see the final shape emerge from clouds of sawdust and swarms of tools. I have never sold a work of my craft. I make gifts of them, and in turn I am drawn up, enclosed by a feeling of great solace that I can make something that pleases and heartens another.

Only the inlaid cross and final finishing remain. I've chosen Australian silky oak for the inlay, a wood that will contrast well with the purpleheart. Where purpleheart is muted, its indigo grain a rippled sea glimpsed from high above, silky oak is brighter, the color of tropical sand on a flat tidal beach: furrows and channels of grain weave languidly through the wood.

I begin the inlay by cutting the shape of a cross, a narrow and modest cross centered on the lid of the box. I use a router, making the cut about an eighth of an inch deep. The motor whines like a cyclone as the carbide bit slices into the wood. I stay away from the pencil lines that mark the edge of the cross. A router removes a great deal of material quickly and easily, but following a straight line on small work is difficult. With larger pieces a router can be set up to follow a straightedge or guide; for something as small as this cross I'm better off using a sharp chisel to incise the edges.

Think of a scalpel and an ax; chisels can function as either. They are either the most refined, elegant tools or a means of butchery, depending on how I work. Most modern hardware-store chisels are designed as small axes, with thick shafts and tough plastic handles able to withstand strong blows from a mallet. It is possible to use the tapered tip as a wedge to force the wood fibers apart, hammering away to get at the right depth and leaning on the tool for leverage. Another approach is to think of the chisel as a small plane designed to slice off a series of thin segments. In terms of the inlaid cross, a more ax-like approach would be to start at the penciled line, hammer the tip of the chisel into the wood the full depth of the inlay, then chip out the waste between the pencil line and the routed cut in large chunks. I'm going the other way: starting at the edge of the router cut, shearing the wood off in tiny increments, without hammering or forcing, until I reach the pencil line and can incise the wood neatly, leaving a smooth face for the inlay.

I make the cross on the bandsaw. Unlike my table-saw, with its voracious, roaring appetite, the bandsaw is modest and restrained. It is less ominous than almost any other power tool. The cutting procedure on a bandsaw goes much more slowly, giving ample time to react if something goes wrong. Because its blade is strung tight, like a musical string, there is music to the work when things go well; problems with the cut can immediately be detected in the landscape of the sound. A bandsaw will never seize and eject the workpiece like a tablesaw. It is more generous in this and other ways.

I return to the box and to my chisels, test-fitting the oversized cross and slowly paring it down so it fits exactly in the inlay. This takes some delicate fiddling. When the fit is precise, I lay down a small bead of glue and secure the piece. The cross is slightly thicker than the depth of the inlay and lies a tiny bit proud of the surrounding top. This excess height allows me to plane down the cross when the glue has dried, leaving it flush. Later, when I run my fingers across the top with my eyes closed, I can just feel the edge of the inlay. When the wax goes on, that edge will be impalpable.

A final inspection of the box is required before finishing. I use a cabinet scraper to smooth a few spots and apply a wash of alcohol to check for any flaws or scratches I've missed. Then I apply a coat of beeswax every day for a week, rubbing the soft wax into the pores of the wood, letting it sit for a few minutes and buffing with a clean cloth. The lustrous sheen of the grain begins to emerge, showing the rippled depth of the wood. It reminds me of polished bone, ancient and dark; scrimshaw caressed by generations of loving hands.

Already this box has the feel of something timeworn, a vessel for a long journey. The artifacts in those Egyptian tombs were designed to facilitate the soul's voyage into eternity, to offer sustenance and companionship, to guide and advise. This small piece in my hands is more modest, yet it, too, is a talisman, a gift of the spirit. There are no answers to the questions posed by guardians of the after-life inscribed here. This object is simpler, fashioned by the energy of receptiveness, designed to protect as well as surrender. Yet there are aspects of this workmanship that would have baffled the ancient Egyptians: the strong mitered joints, without splines, would have been impossible for them. Human magic.

Time to let go, to send this small vessel of my prayers into the earth, where it will be reclaimed and set free. On a warm day, when wind ruffles the colors of the yard, I open the garage door and let bright light and air into the shop. I sweep dark shavings from the floor, wipe the film of sawdust from the worktables, return tools to their niches in various drawers. Elizabeth comes to retrieve the box for its journey to Calgary, where the inurnment ceremony will take place. We cannot all go; I will remain in Vancouver with the kids.

Elizabeth takes the box to the back garden, where evergreen boughs make a canopy over a cedar bench I made. She sits on the bench, head turned to one side, as though a faint, distant sound calls and she has turned her ear toward it. She rests the box in her lap, places Sadie's ashes within, and slides the lid closed. She remains outside a long while, watching shadows deepen in the yard.

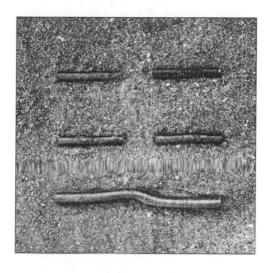

# THUNDER AND LIGHTNING

OUT HERE ON THE ROAD, WITH THE POWER
lines down and early morning light from the sky my only
illumination, I watch a cascade of small branches drift
across the road in a gust of wind. I'm not sure where the
trees have toppled over onto the power lines, but somewhere in this wide countryside the roving wind has struck
with particular vigor. There are no lights on in any of the

small, unassuming homes I pass, places that would at one time have been modest farms but now look as though they're occupied by city commuters. The fields adjoining most of them are derelict. Brown grasses grown above the fence line part and sway as the excited wind rushes through. Though the lights on the highway are out, daybreak has begun to shape the landscape: evergreens vibrant and shining with rainwater, a roadside ditch clogged with a farrago of leaves, a murder of crows wheeling above a barn with a broken back.

Halloween is two days off. The moment of transformation, when the crack between worlds opens just a little wider, when the earth pauses for an instant in its descent toward the darkness of winter to collect both its lights and its shadows for the long journey inward. The weather is always wild this time of year. The air is still warm but with an undercurrent of dissolution: summer trees are bare, rain has begun to wash the forest of its color, gray November waits to wipe the year clean.

During late October the earth finally lets go of autumn's peacefulness. Slowly, building in intensity over a period of weeks, the turbulence of nature unconstrained comes furiously forward: storms and lightning, a ferocious wind, the rolling voice of thunder. Great raging gales race in from the Pacific, flood beachside homes, seize tree branches like immense sails and carry them up into a sky of boiling air.

I stop at a pay phone because I've forgotten the directions to the sawmill, but I discover that without power I can't make a call. As I stand at the edge of the road, trying to decide what to do, I become aware that despite the storm a deepening quiet pervades the morning. The electrical hum of human life has been silenced. Even the wind, rushing down the corridor of the highway, blasting wet paper and pebbles and leaves in its path, seems oddly tranquil.

It is good for me to be out in weather like this. There's a reckless purity at work here, intense and simple, swirling around the silent heart of nature. I am drawn to that intensity, to the thunderous activity of it. It is the pulse of the world. Storms awaken in me a deep sense of aliveness, a fierce clarity that opens a space for what is most true to emerge.

I climb back in the truck and head in what I hope is the right direction. Clouds sweep across the sky, rain comes in fits and starts, thunder rattles the window beside me as I drive. I glimpse a flash of lightning over the trees to the west. I begin counting, using the method I was taught as a boy to gauge the distance lightning is from an observer. Thunder moves at roughly a thousand feet per second, so the delay between flash and crash denotes how far away the actual bolt is. One. Two. Three. And then another shuddering *boom* sweeps over me. Three thousand feet. Not too close, but not entirely safe, either.

The Taoist trigram for thunder shows two open lines atop a single solid line, as though a bolt of lightning has cleft the upper two lines to ground itself on the solid foundation at the trigram's base. In Taoist philosophy thunder represents the movement of energy from formlessness and fluidity toward a fixed ground. Thunder and lightning together beckon the shape of creative endeavor, and their arrival is thus a defining moment in the creative process. They embody the moment of action.

In meteorological terms, lightning and thunder result when the electrical potential between earth and clouds (or between separate clouds) develops sufficiently to allow electrical energy to pass through the insulating barrier of the air. Something happens within the clouds themselves – scientists call it electrical activity, Taoists call it a cauldron of dancing chaos – to supercharge water or ice droplets, polarizing various regions of the clouds, roiling and intertwining them to such an extent that the energy shatters its own container. The charge bursts forth as lightning, which can seek the ground, travel to another cloud, and behave in many unusual ways. Lightning within tornadoes sometimes flashes repeatedly along the tornado's central column, illuminating a magnificent catastrophe spiraling into the sky.

The earth is an electrified body; no one knows how or why. When the energy differential between earth and sky passes a critical threshold, lightning serves to neutralize it in two distinct steps. First comes the leader charge, an electrically negative pulse that descends in a series of steps, forging a path through the air, sometimes traveling horizontally and striking the ground as far as eight miles from the cloud. This is how lightning can strike from a clear blue sky. The leader stroke is invisible, like the cutting edge of a perfect blade.

Sometimes leader strokes move upward instead of down, arcing above the cloud in red and blue flashes, reaching skyward as far as sixty miles to the boundary of the ionosphere. These *sprites* and *blue jets* take the shape of cones, fountains, and dramatic splashes of color that can be seen only from space. Little is known about them; they are utterances in a language we do not understand.

The energy of a downward-traveling leader stimulates a positive charge from the ground, called the return stroke. This is the visible phase of lightning. It is more intense than the leader and travels upward (you can see the direction if you watch closely), passing back along the route created by the leader and terminating in the cloud. The entire process involves hundreds of millions of volts and air temperatures as high as 30,000 degrees centigrade. It is one of the most compelling actions of nature.

Thunder is the voice of lightning. It results when lightning heats up the surrounding air so quickly – within a few millionths of a second – that the air expands with explosive force, creating a sonic shock wave that can sometimes be heard twenty miles from its source. Listen closely to thunder and you'll hear two distinct sounds – a crackling burst from the leader and then, almost instantly, the percussive wallop of the more intense return stroke. The sky speaks and the earth responds.

As creative energies, thunder and lightning bring together heaven and earth, bridge the distance between abstraction and grounding, connect idea with impulse. The moment the bolt touches the earth is the moment of action for any creative endeavor. Something happens, and suddenly the inspirational charge of the work forges a path to decisive action. The time for reflection and consideration is over; invisible forces say *get moving* in voices that are, well, thunderous. It's that leader charge, challenging me to generate a worthy return. And I am always surprised by the suddenness of it, the shock, after incubation and uncertainty and anxiety about the work, of finding myself thrust imperatively down a path whose direction I rarely understand. That's the thing about lightning: it *strikes*. Elusive energies that lie wrapped in the mystery of my work reach out and fill me with movement.

Lightning inspires in me a spontaneous and reckless enthusiasm thoroughly unlike the mood of receptivity – of sacred contemplation – that accompanied the making of Sadie's funereal box. When lightning strikes, my direction is seldom clear, plans are ill-formed, attachment to results is minimal. A flash illuminates a new landscape and

I set out for it, not knowing where it might lead. That's why I'm driving around, a little bit lost, just after sunup during a lovely October storm.

It boils down to this: Bill had some trees he wanted taken down and I thought we could get some good lumber from them. A row of Douglas firs beside his house had grown tall enough to loom over the roof and make themselves vulnerable to strong winds. I don't know why the original owner of Bill's property planted those trees; the eventual danger to the house would have been predictable. Rows of trees or trees planted singly lack the protective buffer offered by a forest and commonly fall over, often onto cars or power lines or across roads. A great many isolated trees are encouraged to grow where there is a boundary or a property line: alongside driveways and roads, in space that's not used much. These places are not natural habitats for evergreen trees. Eventually the solitude gets to them and they just let go into the wind.

The plan to harvest lumber from Bill's trees, which started out not so much as a plan but a vague, abstract impulse toward the pioneering spirit, took shape the previous year when he and I cut down an old beech tree whose roots had begun to dig into his foundation. While we were trimming off the branches on the downed tree, we talked about having it milled into boards. Beech is dense, despite its light, soft color, and is great for woodworking. It is one of the most widely used woods for commercial furniture (especially upholstery frames) and tool handles. Beech also has a reputation in healing practice: salves derived from the tree help heal burns and reduce fevers. Its traditional name, "Mother of the Forest," is well-earned.

The tree went to the mill, and a few weeks later I drove out to Langley for the boards. I loaded far too many into my station wagon, packing them onto the roof and in the tailgate, along the rear seat, angled between the two front seats and pushed up snug against the stick shift, making it impossible to get into reverse. I stuck a few through the front passenger window by way of the back-seat. As I drove home on the highway, they lifted in the wind, shivering with vibration, making the sounds of imminent disaster. But they stayed in place. Every few minutes I slowed the car (why pull off, it only wastes time) and craned my neck out the window to check the roof rack: boards sticking out everywhere, shifting in the wind, bits of bark rubbing off and falling behind, dangerous as hell. But I was not going to make two trips, I pride myself on never having to make two trips, and (with the single exception of the windsurfer that one time coming back from Steveston on the highway, when the mast arrowed forward like some crazy medieval lance and the sail flopped over to cover the windshield) I've never had anything come seriously loose. I've carried loads heavy enough to bend the steel roof rack supports and indent the frame of the car where the rack is fastened, but never two trips.

Lightning inspires recklessness but is generous with luck. I got the boards home without incident and stacked them to dry alongside my house. We didn't end up with much wood, just enough to build a good cabinet, maybe a chair or two, but the experience hooked me on the idea of milling my own lumber – more precisely, getting someone else to mill it for me – and when the row of firs beside Bill's house came down, it was a windfall for my workshop. Not just a single tree this time but twelve, admittedly not of the same caliber as beech but perfectly respectable wood nonetheless. Because of its high weight-to-strength ratio, fir is the wood of choice for beams, roof trusses, and all kinds of construction projects. It works easily, possesses an interesting, undulating grain, and is plentiful in supply. Smells nice, too: fresh and redolent, like pine, but less refined. It's the fragrance of open air, of suddenly emerging from the forest onto cliffs above the ocean, that moment when you realize the depthless sky keeps going, reaches out farther than you can see, and something in you acknowledges your own unfathomable depth.

Fir contains many possibilities. Unlike maple or cherry or walnut, all of which are best suited to fine furniture and cabinetry, fir may be used for almost any woodworking project. I could build a house with it, make furniture to go in the house, use a bit for firewood (but only a little) and distill the bark to make a sweet tea. Even so, twelve trees' worth of fir is a monstrous amount for my small workshop, in which I turn out four or five woodworking projects a year. But the potential of it, the sheer seduction, is too fine to pass up. That's the wonder of lightning and thunder as creative energies: they require only faith in the process and a willingness to be *taken*.

We brought in a faller to take the trees down, possibly saving Bill a hefty insurance claim for a collapsed roof. The logs were laid out in neat rows in front of his house. Unlike the beech tree, which had come to rest conveniently on the driveway, the fir logs were on the other side of the property, forty or fifty feet from the road. Bill's front yard cascades down to the road in a series of three terraces, so we decided to roll the logs. This was great fun, pushing the huge shapes to the edge, watching them tumble off the sharp edge of the top terrace, hang for a moment in the air and then fall six feet to the ground below with a *thwump*. Everything went smoothly, the pile of logs on the lower terrace growing as we worked, until I got a little carried away. Too much spontaneous enthusiasm, I suppose, too much spark. Wanting to see if I could make a log build up enough momentum to leap over both terraces and come to rest at the level of the road, I pushed it as fast as I could, bark spinning across the grass, stubs of branches leaving indents in the ground, and over it went, leapfrogging the logs below, bouncing over the lower terrace, then picking up speed as it rolled toward the road. Toward my car, parked inconveniently in front of the lower terrace. I hadn't counted on that. There was a hushed moment as we stood on the lawn, watching the log trundle toward the front quarter panel of my car, the precise spot I had had repaired and repainted a couple of weeks earlier. Then came the impact, accompanied by the sound of metal clanging indignantly. The car was pushed back a few feet. Even before the impact, I was thinking about how I would explain this to my wife.

I went down and inspected, steeling myself for what I might discover. I had been lucky, unreasonably so. The log had hit squarely on the leading edge of the right front wheel and rolled under the bumper, clearing it by a couple of inches and exerting the brunt of its force against the wheel and shock absorber column. Not a bad place to hit, all things considered: a spot designed to take impact. There was a long, ragged scratch on the column, which turned out to be abraded bark – it came off when I rubbed – and that was all. Recklessness and luck. I climbed in, turned the ignition and tentatively edged the car forward. No new screeches or squeaks, no handling problems. I drove past Bill's property, out of the fall line of future logs, and parked again.

Bill found the incident amusing, my just reward for playing pick-up-sticks with five-hundred-pound logs. A bit later another rolling log sheared off a piece of his rock wall and he was quieter after that. The only other log that got away on us was the one that accidentally went over both terraces, gathered speed as it shot out onto the road (thankfully clear of traffic at that moment), sailed clear across, and headed straight for a new cedar fence someone had carefully built. The fence had a nice clear coat, careful construction: a good job. The log would have smashed right through it but was stopped just short by the only tree within fifty feet. The tree held and the log came to rest quietly in its shade. We went sheepishly over to retrieve it, hoping the neighbor hadn't seen. A real professional outfit we were.

We got the logs down to the road and loaded onto the flatbed of a local trucker, who took them to the mill. A week later I got a call from Karl, the sawyer, to say the milled boards were ready. I had never used Karl's services before, so I gave myself extra time on this stormy morning to find him. But as I'd forgotten his address, and the power to the pay phones was out everywhere I tried, and as I was too shy to ask to use the phone at any of the houses I passed, I ended up driving around in a rented truck thinking about lightning and hurricanes and the weather of creation.

Thunder and lightning are dangerous creative energies. The compulsion to work, the insistent drive to get going, can obscure all other concerns. *I've just got to finish this. Last job of the day, I'll be done in a few minutes.* Such statements often precede injury, mistakes, destruction of the work. Always *one last thing.* It is possible to get carried so completely by the energy of lightning and thunder – there is such a deep reservoir from which to draw – that I am taken over, absorbed completely into my own determined enthusiasm, joyfully pushing the log without noticing the direction it's going. I get lost in the magic of all that energy whirling around inside me, magical and perilous and wonderful. As the *I Ching* says, "When thunder comes, there is alarm, then laughter."

The trick is to survive the strike. When the human body is hit by lightning, the electrical energy tries to find a clear path to the ground; it moves either directly through the core of the body, which is often fatal, or cascades along the surface of the skin and clothing. In the latter case, moisture on the skin conducts the electricity, diverting most of it away from the internal organs and central nervous system. Thus it helps to be wet, fluid. This phenomenon, known as the flashover effect, saves the lives of most strike victims.

Creative energy exhibits the same impulse as lightning. It passes over or through the body, scorching and liberating, sometimes painfully, all that has been restrained, cautious, tentative. It drags me from my slumber, tempting me with visions and dreams of what is possible: a chair made entirely from a single, steam-bent ribbon of wood, a tabletop inlaid with bright stones from the river, copper shimmering at the edge of a cabinet door. And all this from rough wood, hewn raggedly, stripped to its very bones with their hidden light.

When creative lightning enters deep into me, its charge amplifies all my sensations. It runs fiercely up and down my spine. I cannot sit still. Nor can I sleep, because the static inside migrates rhythmically, exploding into shapes as it fills my hands, showing me the poetry hidden in my ribs, the maps of stories that lie along my back. I become an emerging geography of the sacred, sensing the energy pass over that landscape as a searchlight reveals the territory of night.

There is no use in fighting: I must let it pass. Within a day or two the tremors in my fingers diminish, the energy settles into a quieter rhythm and I regain a sense of equilibrium. I can then work with breath that is not frantic, with muscles that do not twitch too quickly into action. And my thoughts slow enough that I can weave them into something useful, I collect them into a long thread that becomes the shape of a project. Yet by the time I can move at a manageable pace, that is, work creatively yet still make supper for my children and walk with my wife in her garden, I know that I have lost the true edge of the work, that invisible edge which is so implacably sharp it cannot be held for long. What I create is always one step removed from what I see in those moments when I am fully possessed by lightning.

Many creative artists describe a different experience of being taken up by the energy of thunder and lightning. It may jangle through them for weeks or months, and is as likely to result in physical illness as great brilliance. The subsequent, inevitable crash is almost always accompanied by deep depression.

Sometimes, when I am especially lucky, the energy of lightning is forgiving. It descends as a gentle, cleansing rain whose drops flash over me and burst into the shapes of flowers as they touch the inviting ground. This is the spiritual engagement of creative possession, when the roar of thunder gives way to the whisper of solace. When the body is buoyed up and carried, a leaf spinning in the autumn air, the flow of movement clear and precise enough that action is only the fulfillment of an inevitable perfection.

Along a stretch of road I've not traveled before, where small farms share the landscape with patches of forest, I begin to notice lights in the windows. The power must be back on. I'm surprised only a mile or so later to find a pay phone at which I am finally able to call home for Karl's address. It turns out I'm quite a ways off, and it takes me another twenty minutes to navigate through truncated streets and winding, disconnected roads to find my destination.

Karl greets me at the door to his ramshackle house. He is grizzled, as I expected, in his sixties, and looks entirely unpredictable. There are several partially completed projects strewn across his front lawn: a gazebo, a deck, a security system with exposed wires dangling from an inert camera. Two concrete cherubs lounge on their sides adjacent to the front door. I imagine Karl is the sort of man in whom the energy of lightning sparks regularly. Tremendous, albeit incomplete, activity and passion for building are everywhere in evidence. Perhaps he enjoys leaving all these projects unfinished. I'm reminded of Michelangelo's sculpture series *The Captives,* in which half-formed human figures struggle to free themselves from solid rock. The pieces were left incomplete, either by accident or by design, and their raw intensity imparts to them a mysterious grandeur. Karl may be a secret genius, intentionally sending an artistic message with his creative detritus. But when I look at him in his faded blue coveralls with the zipper pulled down to his chest, apparently with nothing underneath those coveralls, and there are enough stains and blotches of uncertain origin on them to give the impression of infrequent washing, I abandon my hidden-genius hypothesis and conclude that Karl is just another one of those crusty eccentrics with a generous supply of time, a dearth of social interests, and scores of projects on the go. If this is what the front yard looks like, I wonder what's in his basement.

I follow Karl back to the open space behind his house. He jabbers on about the power outage, how difficult it was to cut up those fir trees by himself, how the estimate he gave me was too low, all the while punctuating his speech with grunts, pauses, repetitions, gesticulations, and snorts. It takes him a while to say much. Yet I find myself falling into a peculiar ease in his presence. Karl is what I would call an old-timer, or an old-world craftsman. He still has the trace of a Danish accent; there's a lilting quality to his voice, a rhythm I've heard from other old-timers I've run across. He talks about practical things, nothing abstract or esoteric: the weather, money, physical work. Basic stuff, talk where I don't have to worry about hidden agendas or double messages or the professional-speak I so often run across, dressed-up jargon without much substance. No, Karl is of the old school, a plain talker, a straight shooter.

I share a camaraderie with these uncommon fellows, a strong resonance for the spirit of craft that shines in them. We're all survivors of countless creative lightning strikes. It's not something that is normally spoken of but rather is felt in the ambience of the interaction, the way a moment is burnished by shared attention to the task at hand, the way steps are followed without having to be recited. This is an unfashionable mode of interaction today – our cultural emphasis on speech often precludes the language of silence – yet many of the richer moments of my life have been spent in the quiet cooperation of physical work. I especially remember the countless hours of childhood I spent working on boats with my brothers and father, cleaning teak and polishing brass and scraping barnacles off hulls, fussing with splices and fishing gear in the still-cold air of early spring, readying a sailboat for long summers.

I remember how my older brother and I discovered what happens when you add a full bottle of catalyst to a lump of fiberglass resin: it begins to bubble and crack, the clear substance turning cloudy from the heat and wafting acrid fumes into the sea air. We'd step back, afraid it might explode but rapt by this rough magic that was like some furious creature fashioning itself on the dock. In five or ten minutes the fumes would subside, the cracking would cease; we'd pick up the warm, solid mass and feel it still humming inside its secret life. I was shaped by those moments the way wood is shaped by the craftsman's hand.

Karl's sawmill is one of the new portable variety, about as long as a bus and half as high. These new mills use a bandsaw blade an eighth of an inch thick with about four feet of exposed, ribbon-like steel. They are much safer than the huge, spinning circular blades of conventional mills and produce as much as a third more wood because of their relatively thin blades. I like these machines; any property owner can mill up and use all the wood cleared for a building lot. Here on the West Coast there's enough wood in the trees taken down to make way for houses to build the houses themselves. But it takes the energy of lightning and thunder, of inspired activity, to make it happen, and most people in our culture have moved far away from an interest in this type of work – skinned knuckles, black pitch underneath fingernails, dirty bark, wet sawdust, and endless sweat. All of which accounts for Karl's coveralls, I suppose.

My wood is stacked in several piles at the far end of the mill. The first thing I notice, after the sheer size of it all, is the color: a plangent diversity of hues ranging from pale yellow to deep orange, striations and waves of rich, brown texture in the grain, dark knots like headlands surrounded by tones of cinnamon, chocolate, bronze, and hazel. Straight from the log, fibers still wet with sap, the wood is alive, intense, true. Possibilities crackle through me.

Karl tells me he has a bad back and shouldn't help me load the wood onto the truck, then spends an hour and a half doing exactly that. All told there's about fifteen hundred board feet, just about enough to frame a small house. Some of it is flitch cut, sawn as a cross-section straight along the log with the bark intact on both edges. Karl has cut most of the boards with one or two straight edges; this will make it easier to run them through a tablesaw or bandsaw later. The average board is two inches thick, a foot wide, eight feet long, and close to a hundred pounds. There are ninety-two boards.

The rain has stopped. Stands of cedar and fir behind Karl's property still swing in the wind, but the storm has begun to move on. I climb up into the bed of the truck and Karl passes me the boards. I try to stack them evenly, keep them level, pile boards of the same width atop one another. This proves to be an unmanageable strategy; there's too much diversity to keep everything neatly arranged. Luckily I've brought gloves, thick leather construction gloves that keep the stiff wood fibers from pulverizing my skin. The wood is so wet, however, that the leather quickly becomes soaked and grows slippery. As I'm positioning a board, the wood slips from my hand and lands squarely on my thumb. I'm thankful that my hands are near-enough numb from the cold and damp because it's a wound that would otherwise have me hopping around, shaking my hand, and shouting *Shit!* I leave my glove on – there's no use stopping, I'll just have to be careful – but I notice over the next few minutes that a dark red stain has soaked through the leather.

The common belief that wearing insulating gloves or rubber-soled shoes will protect one from injury by lightning is false. The energy has passed through miles of resistant air and cannot be stopped by a quarter inch of insulating material. If one is lucky enough to have a lightning strike diverted from the core of the body by virtue of the flashover effect, the usual result is that anything touching the skin becomes instantly superheated and explodes in sundered fragments. Rubber soles dissolve into charred tatters. One is left virtually naked, frightened, and numbly possessed by energies of great power.

When all the boards are loaded, I can't believe the truck will hold the weight. The wood presses right to the edges of the truck bed and rises almost four feet. I climb in the driver's seat, look back, and see that the stack is higher than my head. The top boards are positioned so as to crash through the back window and impale me in the event of a sudden stop. Karl seems confident of this crazy arrangement and merrily waves me on after I pay him for his services, walking alongside the truck as I head back out to the road. And I have the consolation that at least I'm not making two trips.

I drive slowly, taking as many back roads as I can, avoiding traffic, giving myself half a mile to coast to stops. It takes me two hours to cover the twenty miles home. The sun emerges from behind clouds that no longer look menacing. When I pull into the driveway, safe at last, the stress of the trip falls away and I am instantly manic, rushing inside to call Elizabeth and the kids out for a look at my treasures. Alarm, then laughter; thunder rushing across the landscape.

I have not a single idea what to do with all this wood. Yet the first steps are clear: dry and wait. Wood freshly cut from the tree, green wood, cannot be used for most kinds of woodworking. Because of its moisture content, green wood shrinks as it dries; generally not too much – a few percent in width, very little in length – but certainly enough to preclude accurate work. I cannot make precise forms if the material changes in dimension over time. The wood must be dry, down from its current moisture content of thirty or forty percent to about seven percent. That takes, in the case of Douglas fir, about half a year for each inch of wood thickness. Since many of these boards are two inches thick, it will be at least a year before I can use them. A year between the lightning's insistent leader stroke and my own faithful return.

Before I unload the truck I clear a space at the side of the house and lay down some two-by-fours on the wet ground. It's important that air circulates above and below the wood, so I also prepare a number of narrow strips, called sticking, to place between the boards as I stack them. I return to the truck and begin the arduous task of lifting the boards down to the ground, carrying them across twenty feet of lawn, lowering them onto a preliminary sorting pile, then hefting them a final time to lie flat on the developing stack. This time I must do the physical work myself. I don't have the luxury of positioning the boards any which way as I did when Karl and I hoisted them onto the truck. The arrangement must be fairly precise: four boards of equal width and length to a row, each successive row slightly narrower than the last (for stability), sticking placed in three spots along the boards to provide a solid support for the row above. Once I get the rhythm of it, the motions of grasping, slinging, lifting, and placing, the physical intensity of the work shakes me loose from my musings about possible projects and ushers me into the quiet of the body.

Lightning and thunder emerge from silence, from a sky of obscured mystery. They enter and possess, as love possesses. In my own creative practice a particular moment arrives when the work begins to breathe with its own life, when its shapes and turns cannot be claimed entirely by my hand. Lightning grasps, thunder speaks during these moments. And my ability to accomplish creative work, with its emphasis on techniques and devices that are only the shell and not the heart of creative endeavor, depends solely on my willingness to put my own thoughts – sometimes even my own instincts – aside: to be spoken *through*. I must give thunder permission to speak, lightning hands to possess.

The difficulty is always one of listening, of being insulated well enough to survive the strike but still open to the energy of transformation. So many voices strive to be heard, so many demands to take care of the various selves that inhabit me. Yet when I grasp the end of the board, drag it out to where it balances on the tailgate, bring my other hand over and swing the board onto my shoulder, when I walk carefully along the path with the edge of the bark digging into my neck and I cannot recall whether this is the tenth board or the fiftieth, when I am fully enclosed in this moment of balancing and striding and carrying, it is as though my swirling thoughts are laid to rest in the shadow of a larger reality. I become silent. Everything I have ever wanted to know or to be is quieted. And I come to life in a way that I rarely know, a way that reminds me of all the truths I have forgotten, the simplicities I have denied, the struggles I have needlessly engaged. All of this comes wrapped in silence, and drops me into the well of being. I reach back to the formless source of lightning itself.

Then the moment is gone. I catch my foot on a tuft of grass and it rolls my ankle joint over into what my brothers and I used to call a gimp foot. With the extra weight of the board on my shoulder it's a mishap that could twist into a broken ankle. I manage to take the weight off my ankle by relaxing my legs entirely, turn the stumble into a short fall, and in the resulting instant of free motion return my foot to the ground, pushing myself upright again. If I'd been less engaged with my sensory experience, less supported by the cauldron of my body's energy, I would have gone down.

After two hours of puffing and sweating, I discover that the skin on my hands is rubbed raw even through my wet gloves. The stack is four feet wide, twenty feet long, and as high as my chin. The truck's empty loading bed has become a supervision post for Avery, who traverses from side to side, humming. His two-year-old head is perfect and luminous.

Drying green wood in a wet climate involves constructing the stack with enough air circulation that the wood will dry but not exposing it so much that the weather gets in, soaking the fibers and encouraging rot. With this in mind I use a large tarp to cover the top and sides of the pile but leave both ends open. The tarp overhangs the ends a foot or so to direct rain runoff away from the boards. This arrangement will allow air and wind – but not rain – to enter the stack from either end, tunnel through the open spaces created by the sticking and dry the wood effectively. As a final step I retrieve a dozen heavy concrete walkway tiles that Elizabeth removed from the garden path last year when we put down new gravel. Each tile measures a foot square and weighs at least thirty pounds. I distribute them at the top corners of the tarp, along the edges where the tarp meets the ground, anywhere I imagine a strong wind might get some leverage on the fabric and drag it off.

I stop when I'm satisfied the arrangement is sound, but the momentum of the work still flows through me.

I wander around the monstrous pile, not thinking much, just winding down. I notice small stones on the path, watch the way our hedge just touches the tarp in places, pick up flaked-off pieces of bark and toss them down the ravine at the back of our yard. It's only when I finally go inside, take off my gloves, and stretch out on the couch that I notice my deep fatigue. My body starts to shut down, letting go of its impulse to move as the need for movement ceases.

My back and shoulders begin to ache – the hot, swollen ache of overexertion. My thumb, pulverized by a crushing blow and then forced to work hard for hours, feels raw and badly bruised. The juncture between my shoulder and neck, which I've always found to be a stable

niche for carrying lumber but which is inconveniently packed with sensitive tissue, is painfully inflamed. My ankle is sore. I'm wet, tired, and suddenly incredulous. Why did I work so hard? Every movement I make now is accompanied by the rough flavor of discomfort. I just want to be still, somnolent.

I have no idea what to do with all that wood. Yet there it lies, incubating, readying itself for the thunderous moment when I tear off the tarp, seize a piece with wonderfully undulating grain, and carry it off in service of some new crazy idea, knocking the drainpipe at the side of the house loose as I swing around the corner into the shop.

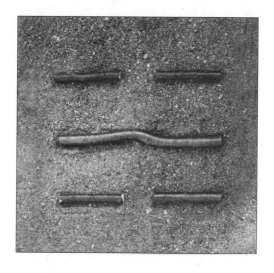

## 4

# DEEP WATER

TODAY THE WORK IS TENSE, RUSHED, POSSESSED
of a sharpness I feel inside, as though I might crack open
from the cold. The heater is cranked up, I've opened the
door to the adjoining furnace room, and I'm wearing a
thick fleece jacket. But these measures barely soften the
hard edge of the cold in the shop. It's December, and the
sun shows itself so infrequently there are days I wonder
if it's come up at all. Elizabeth tells me I should come in,
my shop is not comfortable enough to use during the

winter, I should leave it all until spring when I can open the garage door and let the glorious morning light sweep through. She's right, it is too cold. My hands are red and puffy; the tools seem less forgiving, the wood brittle.

Yet I persevere. This is supposed to be fun, and I won't allow a bit of physical discomfort to get in the way of my forced enjoyment. After all, I'm excited about this project, the marimba that I'm hoping will make the wood sing with a new voice. Marimbas are musical instruments of African and Latin American origin, similar to xylophones but with wooden keys that produce a sonorous ululation of notes. I've never made a project such as this, and the novelty of it, the challenge of enticing the wood to call out with its own rhythm, has me working every night, battling the cold, my little shop lights defiantly brightening my small space against the wide, indifferent darkness.

Sounds of the world travel far on the chill air: the crack of brittle bark in the forest, the steady drip of water falling from the eaves onto the tarp-covered fir beside the house, the slam of a car door shutting out the wind. The lights and colors of fall have given themselves over entirely to the clear sounds of winter, the physical austerity of it, and my body responds haltingly. I watch the wood less and feel it more. My hands are immersed in the sensations of the shop, steel tools and a concrete floor and boards that wake me with their intensity as I touch them.

The work I do in winter is like a journey on a wide, dark sea. I slow, wrapped in expectation, as if waiting for the great bell of the sky to be struck. Winter lays bare what is fundamental, strips the world of adornment, beckons me to wait and listen for the voice of the invisible. It was once thought that a great silence would allow one to hear the music of the spheres; winter encourages that silence, leads me down to an elemental realm of dark sea, dark stone, dark shore. And I listen, trying to understand the unspoken language.

My kids have a small marimba, nothing fancy, yet the music it produces is surprisingly resonant. And I thought, *I could make one of these, could probably even improve on it.* The joints could be tighter, the keys more finely cut, the finish refined. Soon enough I was out in the shop, making plans, sawing wood, embarking on another grand expedition of craft. But I'm out of my depth: that's soon apparent. Sure, I bought a book on instrument design and looked at a few marimbas, even took some measurements to get my bearings on how to proceed. But a map is not the territory, and I don't get far before I start to wonder why this seemed like a good idea.

It begins with the keys: selecting a number of woods, making a key from each, testing for the richest sound. There's no guideline about which woods work best for marimba keys. Each has a distinctive character and makes music that reflects its nature, its experience of growing in the forest. A key may make a gentle sound that sustains for four or five seconds, like a weathered trunk yielding to the wind, or it may possess a more distinctive ring, sharper, clearer, but more quickly fading, like a woodpecker hunting deep in the tree.

I plan to make roughly half a dozen preliminary keys to test for the optimum combination of wood species and key shape. Because I've read that exotic hardwoods can work well, I select several pieces from the small inventory of cocobolo, purpleheart, and padauk that I keep in my shop, being careful to waste as little as I can, knowing I might use only one of the test keys in the final instrument. The others will be put aside, odd-shaped remnants difficult to use in other projects. I keep such offcuts in a bin that still contains discarded pieces from my first project, the cedar bench, for which I twice miscut the curved rails. Occasionally, as I rummage through the bin looking for a piece that's just right for a jig or a clamping aid (a caul, to be precise), I come across those cast-off rails and wonder how, in the depth of my ignorance of the craft at that time, I made anything at all. Yet the bench is still there, weathering the seasons in our backyard, joints still tight, lines still true.

At first glance, making a marimba key seems like a straightforward procedure with a couple of basic requirements. A key that is too large, say anything over two inches wide and eighteen inches long, vibrates at a

*A marimba key (seen here from the side, with mounting holes) vibrates at a pitch derived from its size and shape: longer keys make lower tones, shorter keys higher ones. The curved cut underneath enhances the resonance; material is removed from there to lower the pitch. Shortening the key, or shaving a portion from its end, raises the pitch. It's all quite straightforward, and as frustrating as rowing with one oar.*

frequency too low for making music. A key that is too small, about eight inches long or less, results in a tintinnabulation too high to be pleasing. I make my test keys in the middle range, about an inch and a half wide, twelve inches long, and an inch thick. Then I add a wide, curved cut halfway through the underside of each key. This lowers the basic tone of the key (the fundamental) and enhances its resonance. As I work, I become aware of instrument-making as an activity distinct from other kinds of woodworking. Most woodcraft involves searching for a visual aesthetic, laboring with the body to shape that which pleases the eye. In instrument-making, conversely, one searches for the most pleasing sound, favoring auditory clarity over visual beauty. It is a realm not only of aesthetics but *audiosthetics*.

This is where I run into trouble. I can make an attractive key, one with clean lines, a smooth, curved underside, and grain that flows well with the shape and size of the key. But I discover that I have no way of assessing the sound the key makes. I line up four or five on a set of foam pads I've rigged up for testing purposes and tap them in sequence: *bing, bong, bung.* Are those good sounds? Are they musical? Do they make notes like the notes on a marimba, or on a piano? And although I am aware that the sounds from each key are different – I can hear the distinctiveness – I cannot tell which tones are higher or lower. I tap a key, then another, going back to the first again and trying to listen for the higher tone. The first key sounds higher, then the second. I tap a third for contrast, and they all sound the same.

Since the keys are made from different woods, perhaps the variances in tone are due to their different properties. To find out, I make another four keys, all of purpleheart. I shape the largest to be eighteen inches; the smallest is ten. When I test them I can clearly discern the lower notes from the higher, which is a definite improvement. Now I need to know the specific note each key produces so I can create a musical scale. I take my kids' marimba into the shop and compare the sounds of its keys with my test keys, looking for similar notes. Once again the sounds blend together, making it impossible to distinguish the tonal differences. I don't get a particular sense of the pitch rising or falling; at least I don't perceive it as a vertical scale. I simply hear the sounds: pleasant, sonorous shapes in the air, brushing past me and dwindling into the winter day.

I enjoy the sounds, and I play around just tapping keys, not looking for a particular tune but listening to the results of an amazing discovery: wood sings. Every woodworker knows that wood speaks, but this singing – it is like discovering your arms can also be wings.

I ask around and discover that there's no such thing as tone deafness, just a lack of ear training. My inability to hear the scale of the notes is simply perceptual innocence. Armed with this revelation, I rush down to the music store on a rainy night and purchase two slender steel tuning forks as reference notes. Back in my car I strike the forks one at a time against the steering wheel and hold them to my ear. They produce clear, resonant notes, an A and a C, which sustain for close to ten seconds. Lovely. But when I hold them up at the same time, one against each ear, I can't tell which is higher. I have to check the tiny letters inscribed in them to be sure.

I return to the shop and try to compare the sounds of the tuning forks with those of my marimba test keys. They seem so different, one set produced by metal and the other by wood, that I can't discern which keys most closely match the forks. Everything makes its own sound: distinct and resonant yet secluded. There is no harmonious choir of notes. Which is well and good if all I want is a bunch of separate keys on my workbench. But I am trying to make an instrument, something that will produce an even scale of notes, an object to sing with harmony. So far I have quite a few keys made from expensive, endangered woods, a couple of nice-sounding tuning forks, and no results. And I don't even know how to get on track. I have no map, and though I'm used to exploring in this craft, watching and discovering as I go, it's not my eyes that I need but my ears, and they seem to wander all over, finding many delights but no clear channel to follow. I'm starting to feel a little lost.

In Taoist philosophy the energy of deep water begins with disorientation, with a sense of being drawn onward in ways that are uncomfortably challenging. In creative terms, deep water lies at the heart of authentic work. There is a fashionable notion that involvement in creative work, in the spirituality of creativity, will lead not into shadow but toward a great light, toward happiness or self-improvement or refinement of one's energy and purpose. Yet the creative journey also leads to a shadow-land of doubt, fear, frustration, and depression. It passes directly, unavoidably, across ominous stretches of water where destructive, threatening forces lie in wait. In my truest creative work I must be taken apart by those forces, relieved of my carefully constructed masks, and laid bare to see how restless and fugitive I really am.

I hang around in the shop for a few days, halfhearted at best, trying to make sense of this whole procedure. I'm steadily going through my supply of good wood, it's getting colder every morning, and the kids, virtually housebound from the rain, never give me more than ten minutes of actual working time. Both Rowan and Avery are quite capable of playing happily for at least an hour; they do so regularly when I am washing dishes or making supper or cleaning up toys. For them, the main thing is that I be in sight, immediately accessible. As long as I stay in the same room with them, I can find two or three hours in a given day to accomplish household tasks. Usually this means puttering around the kitchen while they play in the adjoining family room. But as soon as I go through the door into the shop – either announcing my exit or sneaking off quietly, it doesn't matter – the sounds of bedlam come echoing down the hall: wailing and crying, screaming matches over the ownership of toys, plaintive moans for food or juice as though the fridge has been bare for weeks.

Sometimes I encourage them to come into the shop with me. They both have small kits of plastic tools – saws, hammers, screwdrivers – and I help them work with offcuts. Last year Rowan made a couple of hanging mobiles with plane shavings and bits of string. Originally I thought that bringing the kids along would give me more time to do hand work (I don't use power tools when they're around), but the regret wasn't long in coming. The kids have the idea that sawdust is the most entertaining thing in the shop. They make little piles with it, spread it around the floor, drop it into bins already filled with equipment, throw it at each other by the fistful, dump it on each other's heads. I fill a thirty-gallon plastic garbage container with sawdust twice a month and gather it up only when it becomes a serious hazard on the floor, so they have plenty of ammunition. What do I expect, letting loose a two-year-old and his five-year-old sister in a giant sandbox of shavings?

It's a good thing a marimba key takes only about ten minutes to make, because that's all the dedicated time I have during these long, dark days. Elizabeth helps when she can, diverting the kids from the shop and sometimes taking them out for a couple of hours when I'm desperate for working time. But it's a slow, frustrating haul. Deprived by the cold of backyard diversions, the kids turn to Elizabeth and me as virtually their sole entertainment. Sometimes, when they are jumping up and down on my last nerve, I envy the isolated artists, the ones whose solitary lives offer endless stretches of time and freedom in which to work. Craft so often demands selfishness, a resolute focus on one's own ideas and plans. Attending to the needs of others falls distantly behind. Parents, conversely, are required constantly to surrender their own needs in favor of their children's. Negotiating the balance between sacrifice and self-interest in relation to one's children is the most creatively demanding task available to a human being. It is far more difficult, by any measure, than the personal odyssey of the artist.

Which, I suppose, raises the question of why we often look to artists as teachers of society and to art as a repository of wisdom. Shouldn't we look to parents instead, and to children? Working as an artist or craftsman can be a substitute proof that one is really in the world. But being a true parent requires that one be firmly, inescapably, rooted in the soil of life.

All this loose talk gets me no closer to making a marimba. The keys are still there, indecipherable. I'm wasting time. The workshop is cold and damp. There's mess everywhere, sawdust and discarded tools and offcuts drifting into little piles at the foot of the bandsaw. Yet I can't get motivated to clean up, don't seem to be going anywhere, there's not enough time to get anything done. It really is cold. And now I'm complaining, as though this craft forces unmanageable demands on my otherwise pristine life.

I decide to give up for a while, let myself drift until something nudges me back on track or convinces me to abandon the project altogether. I am adrift, far out in the sea of winter without any means of movement. If I remain this way too long, waiting for the puzzle of the keys to resolve itself, I will likely be drawn into the depths where depression, disillusionment, and their many companion shadows lie. I'd rather move forward, yet I'm aware that in my creative work there are times when the momentum departs, energy dwindles, the safe passage vanishes, and all comes to a shuddering halt. Sometimes what I need, the particular flavor of truth I seek, can be found only in the deep water.

I stay out of the shop for close to a month as the flurry of Christmas gives way to a new year. A muted snowfall in early January has me out clearing the driveway, desultorily, the blade of the shovel ringing in the cold air as it scrapes the pavement. Its wooden handle is remote and unyielding as I plow away mechanically, distantly aware that my relationship with tools, with wood, has been stalled by my impasse with the marimba. Not enough knowledge, no discernible track to follow. I begin to sink.

One minute she was there on the boat deck, shouting and crying with a look of mingled rage and terror, desperate; the next, she had jumped over the side into the dark water. It happened quickly, and was so unexpected that we all rose up in a chorus of panic. My younger brother began to cry, the confusion and madness of it swelling inside him. He was only four – what was he to make of his mother plunging into the frigid waters? My father handed the wheel to my elder brother and jumped in the dinghy. My brother stood there, small and frightened, his cold hands gripping the bright steel. He brought the boat around as my father pulled her up from the water and into the dinghy, her jacket sodden, her hair wild. I didn't want to look at her, not knowing how to respond to such violent upheaval. It would have been an intrusion into her own private world of despair. And I hated her for living in that world. My father turned the boat back to the dock and helped us unload our bags. My mother ran up the ramp and disappeared. My father drove us home before going to look for her. No one spoke. I was nine.

My mother never came up from that dive, though it took her twenty years to complete her long sweep into oblivion. The water laid claim to her, never letting go; it kept drawing her down until there was nothing left but to surrender to that cold embrace. We followed her down, of course, into the dark labyrinth.

The seascape of constant stress and upheaval that I walked through with my mother was not graceful, yet it was among the most powerful journeys of my life. Through her I learned deeply about what is inevitable in true creativity: descent to the abyss. The truth most often lies hidden there, and holding out long enough to glimpse it – without drowning – is a serious race indeed.

It takes just over a minute for a drowning person to take a deep breath of water. No matter how desperately the breath is held, waiting, clutching for the surface, there comes a moment – the racing heart of panic brings it more quickly – when the danger of imminent unconsciousness from oxygen deprivation causes instinct to override volition. It's the body's last gamble: holding the breath much longer will result in certain disaster, and a quick breath might coincide with the availability of oxygen. One final bet, no matter how ill-advised, is usually a good idea when there's nothing left to lose. As the closure of the aperture of consciousness approaches, the lungs heave, the mouth opens, and water makes its ultimate trespass. This entry of the catastrophic is called the break point.

Near the end of January it becomes clear that I must dive into the work again or risk losing my motivation altogether. The break point has arrived. Cutting my losses and moving on to a new project feels like a failure of courage – I need to *know* how to decipher the resonant language of the wood. I need to understand the song. No more holding, no more waiting.

I spend the last week of January in San Francisco, where I get my hands on some California redwood. I've heard it works wonderfully for marimba keys. Perhaps the keys possess a deep song, what the poet Lorca called *cante jondo,* because of the particular qualities of the wood. After all, redwoods are among the largest and oldest trees on the planet; some were alive well before the time of Christ and along with the other conifer species possess the most complex DNA on the planet.[3] More complex than our own, for reasons that are obscure only until the wood and the hand begin to speak.

I purchase an eight-foot board, enough for twenty keys, and have it cut into eighteen-inch lengths. I cram the pieces into my luggage; they don't quite fit. Several ends stick out the top of my carry-on bag, and as I make my way home through airports and in shuttle buses, I notice the sorrel, almost pink hue of the wood. It reminds me of the first tendrils of sunrise, sweeping the eastern sky with light.

I abandon my efforts at ear training, tuck the tuning forks away at the back of my workbench, and buy an electronic tuner. I hold the magic little machine beside a key, strike the key, and wait for the LED readout to show me the exact pitch of the sound along with its assigned note. So far so good. It's a lazy work-around for the problem of my ill-trained ear, but it provides the jumpstart I need.

The redwood shapes nicely into two test keys. I place them alongside the keys of padauk and purpleheart and tap them all with the mallet, listening, watching the readout on the tuner. The hardwoods possess a clearer tone but the redwood is more sonorous, sounds more forgiving, sustains a bit longer. Of all the woods I've tried so far it seems the best choice. With more than a little chagrin I place all the other test keys aside, hoping that I can use them in other projects but knowing their odd shapes and relatively small size will likely mean a long residency in the offcut bin. I keep wondering if I could have found a way to be less wasteful.

I fashion fifteen keys between eight and sixteen inches long. The instrument book informs me of the length each key should be to produce a sound one note higher than its companion.[4] Once shaped, each key requires fine-tuning with sandpaper on its underside or edges to bring out its exact note. Things are starting to improve, the winter seems less indifferent. The feeling of being dragged down is starting to dissipate.

I finish tuning six keys and playfully run the mallet up and down the even-tempered scale, thinking how easy this is becoming. I'm almost back in known territory. Then I take the completed keys inside to show Elizabeth and leave them on the kitchen counter while we eat supper. By the time I get around to showing off my prowess as a musical instrument maker, the keys have warmed up to room temperature, the wood has taken on different tonal properties, and I realize, with growing despair about this entire project, that the keys are no longer in tune. The scale sounds rough and unbalanced, the notes a haphazard mix of noise.

It is difficult to get back on track and then be broadsided by unforeseen problems. I don't seem any further ahead. How am I supposed to tune the keys, and hold them in tune, if every time I move the damn things to

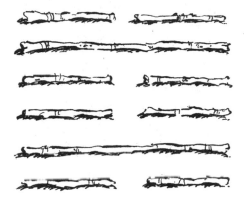

*Mastering Pitfalls*

*"Don't ruin and abandon yourself and become useless to the world just because you may have little in the way of blessings . . . The goal is near at hand."*

(I Ching commentary on hexagram 29)

another room all my efforts are wiped out? I can't remember when a project has been so frustrating. And I'm still near the beginning; I have the frame to make as well, and the suspension system for the keys. And finishing. What a mess this is all turning out to be.

The *I Ching* offers many strategies for finding safe passage through the deep waters. Several are collected under the heading "Mastering Pitfalls," which is represented by the image of two deep-water trigrams; difficulty upon difficulty. The commentary emphasizes truthfulness and perseverance: accepting the reality of descent, preparing to meet the hidden faces of the deep. Thus it helps to be honest with myself and acknowledge my growing hatred of this project, this quaint little instrument that began as an exploration and is turning into a disaster. I must also believe in the danger of it, the way it threatens to stall the good feelings I hold for my craft. And despite these I must keep going, "without hypocrisy or deception, practicing truly," as the Taoist commentators urge.

Perhaps I am sinking into the deepest waters and my burst of enthusiasm was nothing more than the involuntary breath of a drowning person. Perhaps there's nothing I can do to prevent this project from taking me down. If prior experience is any indication, I should just go with it.

After the break point, when water invades the body, the bloodstream is deprived of whatever remaining oxygen might be in the lungs. The brain begins to shut down, awareness becomes irretrievably distant, muscles cease their spasmodic flailing. The surface dwindles, sinking accelerates.

Some of the deepest creative work derives from affliction, from the racking pain inflicted by life's indifference. I see clearly, with the final look of my childhood innocence, that my mother will truly drown, clawing at the bright bonds of my family as she goes, dragging us down, grasping us with such furious desperation that we will eventually be fractured, worn almost to nothing. I glimpse the later moments of horror and terror, the long road of many years of secrets, violence, and confusion. And at the end, when our last chances for making peace as a family come and go, we are left with only the grief of our inevitable disappointment.

Creative energy lies buried in the heart of the wound. And the creative path requires that I redeem myself through that wound, take my deepest wisdom from it. That's the way it is. There's no fullness without first that rough, implacable opening as the world pries into you with its darkest shapes.

I keep working, making more keys, leaving the issue of final tuning for later. I try not to get carried away with the philosophical or spiritual resonance of the word *surrender* but keep focusing on the actual work, what it presents each moment physically and emotionally: the challenge to keep going, even when the results seem distant, the recognition that I might waste not only the test keys but also this lovely redwood, the persistent doubt and anxiety, the memory of those childhood days of deep water this project has revived. The keys come alive with strange music in my work, blending their harmonies with the sounds of my feeling.

Other, more disturbing concerns arise: that I might become stranded in the deep water, trapped like my mother in an endless whirlpool of descent; that in the oppressive darkness I might lose my way and let go of this craft that has so nurtured and challenged me; that my creative work, bereft of light, adrift in the shadow of this incomplete and persistently difficult endeavor, might slide into purposeless apathy; that I might forget myself, and in forgetting abandon whatever creative contribution I could have made. I might just forget the whole thing and live another, quieter life, haunted by what I should have done.

The curious thing about wood is that it does not allow me to give up. It cajoles and prods, it demands that I keep my end of the bargain and bring out its hidden forms. At times it even taunts me, this ancient material possessed of its own craftiness. I'm not sure exactly how the wood makes its demands — saying that it *speaks* is only a shorthand for something more elusive and mysterious. Seeking to define it is only a game of words.

From some musician friends I discover that the tuning of many instruments fluctuates; the secret is to keep them in an environment of stable humidity and temperature. I need to keep the shop warmer, at room temperature, but around the time I learn this the heater breaks down. The only warmth now comes from the halogen lights and the fleece jacket I wear. I pretend it's warm enough to work. Another snowstorm hits and I am forced to evacuate the shop. The cold is just too much. I catch myself hoping for a lightning strike, something to jolt me into action, to burn away this suffocating paralysis. But lightning is not one of the gifts of the deep water.

February passes. I finish all the keys, working in fits and starts between spells of intense cold. The work feels rudderless, even though the solution to my tuning problem seems straightforward. I buy a new heater and warm up the shop, but I hardly go in at all. I'm sinking, somewhere between the surface and the ocean floor. I wonder about the craft I've chosen, try to remember why it's so important. I wish the sun would come out, or another storm would break the monotony. But nothing. Rain and gray and the feeling I've lost the thread.

Then, in mid-March, one of my drowning eyes pops open. I've been working exclusively on the marimba keys, trying to complete them before designing the frame. A dream of a Japanese bridge stays with me through a damp morning and suddenly, just swimming out of the black water, comes an idea for the frame: the delicate curve of a bridge, arching upward to support keys that can be a walkway across the deep water. I make a simple sketch, which is about as far as I ever get with design, and an inkling of excitement thrums through me. The depths have offered me clear passage, a gift from the dark waters. I'm reminded of Rua, the Tahitian god of craftsmen, whose name means "abyss."

There are spirits in the deep water, phantasms that appear only to the drowning and to submariners of surpassing skill. Down deep, where the water is colder than ice but under too much pressure to freeze, where the darkness is absolute and hydrothermal vents expel poisonous toxins in black, acidic spumes – far down, in an environment most remote from us – there is exotic, pristine, awesome life, the oldest life of this world. The abyss is home to the most primordial forms, and they are guardians of a great secret: dark, still waters are the sanctuary of the soul.

Apparitions both angelic and bestial inhabit this seascape of elemental dreams. The long-nosed chimera, also known as the ghost shark, has a dorsal spine so venomous a single touch can kill. The male of the triplewart sea devil, with its bioluminescent tendrils, chews through the skin of the female and fastens himself on, merging their bloodstreams in a bizarre sexual dance.

This pantheon of monstrosities is large indeed. The viperfish boasts fangs so long they extend beyond its mouth, arcing upward toward its deep eye sockets. Its abyssal companions include the fangtooth fish, also known as the ogrefish, and the group of gulper fish that can swallow prey larger than their own bodies. One of their number, the black swallower, draws its curved, needle-like teeth slowly over the entire length of its trapped victim. And there are creatures of mythological heritage: *Vampyroteuthis infernalis* (literally "vampire squid from hell") has the largest eyes of any animal, and the basket starfish, belonging to the family *Gorgonocephalidae,* is named after the snake-haired Gorgons of Greek mythology.

But just as the winged horse Pegasus emerged from the bloody remains of the Gorgon, the deep is a place not only of nightmares. Elegant swordfish travel the wide range between deep water and inviting surface. Among the many varieties of lantern fish, which give off their own shimmering and refulgent light from within, are those that journey to within a few feet of the surface at night and return to the abyss at daybreak. Their bodies are richly colored in glistening blue and iridescent silver. Vast arrays of them have appeared beneath shipwrecked sailors drifting in the north Pacific, hovering just below the surface, watching or waiting or wondering – no one knows – and vanishing as the rescue boat draws near.

The deep is home to ten million species of life, far more than are known to exist on land. Only the drowned and the recklessly brave have the opportunity to enter that hidden realm where no light shines. Yet, like the lantern fish, one can undertake that far journey and return.

Above my workbench, hanging in front of my first-aid kit on the upper shelf, is an old black fishing float, a long wooden ovoid with a large central hole through which a net rope once passed. I found it on the beach, near my grandmother's summer home, around the time my mother jumped from the boat. My father helped me fashion on it the shape of a rudimentary face: the curve of a shell glued on to make a mouth, eyes animated with gold and silver hobby paints, a segment of frayed rope through the hole making a shock of wild hair. I made that float into a charm, a deep-water talisman that stayed with me through the turmoil of those years. And still it watches, its black, elemental form like a creature of the abyss come to make a companion of the light. Who knows what forces come to our aid in the deep water? We never quite see their elusive faces but rather sense the accompaniment of a guiding gentleness that ushers us onward.

I decide to use pine for the marimba frame. I have a gen-erous supply in my shop and if I run into further trouble it's inexpensive to replace. The only drawback to pine is its softness, though it has not always been a very soft wood. At one time, a hundred years ago and more, the forests of North America were tightly packed with trees that grew more slowly as a result of diminished light and space. Growth rings on those old trees were closer together and the wood, therefore, was much stronger. In those days one could use pine for the hull of a ship. Today, forests have been thinned dramatically and pine is among the softest woods, easy to saw but difficult to shape with precision.

In creative terms, the only safe way out of the depths is to let the darkness slowly release its grip, to glide upward in a slow, easy arc. Creative crisis or creative illness usually happens when one tries to surface too quickly or cannot surface at all. Sometimes one is caught between the terrible inertia of the deep and the reckless rapture of surfacing. This is what psychologists used to call manic-depressive illness. It is the cycle of the gifted artist: to descend fully into the depths where ancient secrets lie, partake of the original dreams of the world, and then arrow upward to burst gloriously from the water, flanks sparkling in the sun like a great swordfish, hanging for a moment like a dazzling fire poised on the palm of the sea. But only for a moment.

Surfacing without incident requires evading predators at every depth. The tablesaw, ravenous shark that it is, reminds me of this as soon as I begin to shape the parts for the frame. Halfway through my first cut the saw seizes the workpiece in its jaws and flings it back at me. A whistling blur rushes past my ribs, arrows across the shop, and punches through the wall twenty feet away. A small cloud of wallboard dust settles to the ground. I can see the exposed wiring of the house through the hole. *Careful.*

The mishaps continue. Gluing up the frame panels goes poorly: the grooves on the curved frame legs are difficult to cut and require completion by hand; an end panel fails to seat correctly, resulting in a flurry of panic to correct the problem as the glue is drying. But I've come to expect such hurdles with this project. I begin to take them in stride, as though the deep water must extract a toll for allowing a glimpse of its astonishing shapes.

The Japanese bridge I saw is among the most elegant forms I've attempted to reproduce. It is a gift of the abyss.

And I am surprised to discover, upon measuring where the curved legs meet the uprights of the frame, that the angle is seventy-two degrees, the "ruling number" of ancient sacred geometry. It is the number that unlocks the esoteric religion of astronomy to which the ancient Egyptian culture was devoted, and here it is, like a secret code in my marimba, come back like a stowaway from the black depths.

The frame goes together in stages through March and April as winter slowly retreats. The air feels more damp than cold, the street at night more slick than hard. Scents of spring ride the air, but like the music of the marimba keys, their identification eludes my untrained nose. The shop can now be kept at room temperature, and I tune all the keys to within a hair of what the machine points to as the perfect note. The suspension system – thin colored rope threaded through steel tubing, O-rings at the rubbing points to dampen vibration – is an odyssey of experimentation. I become a metalworker for a few days, grinding and drilling material that glows red-hot under duress, stains my hands the color of dark stone, and, more than once, spits out a tongue of flame.

Prior to mounting the keys I apply a coat of rubbing varnish to the frame – just one coat so as not to impede the amplifying function of the panels. I leave the keys themselves unfinished after discovering on one of the test pieces that a single coat of oil affects the tuning by as much as half a note. I polish the keys instead, using fine abrasive paper, until the grain shimmers, languid.

I thread the keys through the arrangement of cord and steel tubing, adjust the tension – and then it's done. I find the small mallet I've been using all along, the one I lifted from my kids' marimba, the one that's been buried beneath flakes of ground steel and pine shavings since I began the frame. It feels cool in my hand, expectant.

I tap the keys, poised now alongside their companions as a choir might arrange itself. The sounds are like bells shaped by hands of water, low and soft as the whispering voice of the sea at twilight.

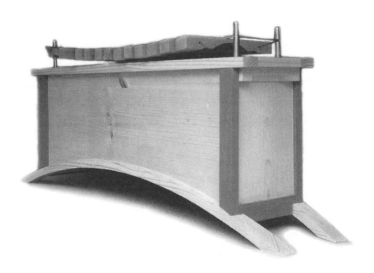

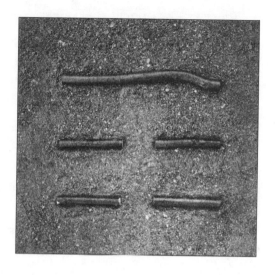

# MOUNTAIN

THIS LITTLE STANLEY BLOCK PLANE, THE FIRST woodworking tool I owned and still one of my favorites, has a surprising heft. I cradle it in my left palm, sole up, where the contours of the lever cap – the assembly that holds the blade in place – fit neatly into the two deep furrows, what palm readers call the head and heart lines, that mark the deepest cleft of my skin. My hand feels pleased, as always, to discover something that fulfills it so precisely. I can just see my fate line tracing its way over the edge of my palm and disappearing between my first and second fingers. My fingers themselves are curled slightly, nestling the plane. Small scars trace the landscape of my knuckles, souvenirs from countless unremembered mishaps with fishing hooks and carving knives and pavement. This left hand, the central instrument for my interactions with the world, has been bitten by frost and by dogs, scraped along gravel roads, burned while setting bonfires with gasoline, made to suffer innumerable indignities. Most of the skin on the palm and pads of the fingers was once abraded off during a long and desperate slide down a gritty rope after a climbing harness broke. The hand was immersed many times in buckets of acetone and xylene and lacquer thinner in the days before anyone thought much about how toxic that stuff was. It is the hand that first reached for the man who lay face down in the water after he jumped from the bridge, and the one with which I greeted both my children, their first touch outside the womb.

My right hand is less supple than the left, rougher, simpler. It didn't seem to mind when a shard of coral from a bodysurfing accident lodged itself alongside the third finger, inhabiting that warm space for over a year before sliding out. And at the lake, when I inadvertently pierced the thumb with a homemade arrow, it never complained but let the wound heal quietly into the delicate white ridge that lies there today. There's not much of a thumb joint left on my right hand after too many unreasonable demands made by ski poles and water-ski bars and sailing ropes. I seem never to have learned there are limits to how long my thumb can lock my grip and hold all my weight. Nowadays, if I don't apply too much pressure, my right thumb works fine, but if I try to lift a phone book by its spine or carry a two-by-four across the shop with a single, overhand grip, I can cripple the joint for a month.

I rotate my left hand, turn the sole of the plane downward, place it on the wood and bring my right hand across to cover the left: for support, solace, camaraderie. Together they will push the plane, reaching out again for that territory of the new, reminding me that my hands – more than my breath or my eyes or my mind – have shaped my life.

My hands guide the plane along this fine, straight-grained maple as the blade lifts small shavings into the throat and twists them into a myriad of spiraling shapes. The sharp edge slices the wood into ribbons of parchment rolled tight, a secret testament. The test of good planing is to be able to unroll the shavings onto an open book and read through them to the text beneath. If the shavings are thin enough – a few thousandths of an inch – the words magically appear as though written on the wood, just as they did when we were kids writing in lemon juice and holding the paper over a candle flame. The magic of memory is only one of many spells woven by the work of hands.

Occasionally I adjust the depth of the cut to take the finest shaving possible, working toward a surface that is dead flat and shimmering with smooth, sheared wood fibers. Block planes are not usually the tools of choice for final smoothing, designed as they are for end grain and the simple chamfering of edges. I have a smoothing plane, much larger and more precise than this little Stanley, but for a workpiece this small, about three by eight inches, the block plane feels just right. In fact, I find many reasons to use this plane when another might be more suitable. I even use it for the delicate task of jointing boards while my jointing plane sits idly by, patiently enduring the long periods of finicking and adjusting, knowing it could make short work of the whole thing, waiting for the inevitable moment I discover the joints are not quite right and finally – grudgingly, haltingly, peevishly – admit that the jointing plane will do a better job. There's something about this little block plane, the way it has so faithfully stayed with me, transmitting the feel of the wood to my hands as though it were an extension of my own body. This is not to be taken lightly in a tool. There are rich rewards in finding the hands themselves taking another shape, flowing out into the world, discovering how it feels for steel to slice and for wood to reveal its hidden shape.

My hands deliver tiny insistent messages to my arms as I work, nudging them to move this way or that, drawing strength down through finger muscles that stretch far up into the arm. Encircle your left forearm with your right hand, wiggle your left index finger, and you'll feel the muscle moving all the way up to your left elbow (there are actually two muscles involved, on either side of the arm, one to pull the finger up and another to pull it down again). The fingers have a long reach indeed, and they take advantage of that reach to accomplish the most powerful and delicate tasks. With practice, rock climbers develop the ability to suspend their full weight for short periods from the tip of an index finger. At the other end of the spectrum, craftsmen learn to distinguish surface variations in wood that are invisible to the eye – variations as small as several molecules, the thickness of a single coat of wax applied to the sole of a plane.

The perceptual accuracy of the human body routinely exceeds that of the finest instruments we can devise. The eye can detect a single photon. And the well-trained ear is capable of hearing sound variations undetectable by machines. I depend on machines; I'm not going to be throwing clogs into them anytime soon. But no matter how advanced they become, the important work in my craft is done by hands: careful selection, by sight and by touch, of woods and grain, the refinement of softly eased edges, the clarity and smoothness of hand-rubbed surfaces.

The powerful lever of my elbow opens and closes as I push the plane along the wood and retrieve it for another stroke. High up my arm two opposing muscles act as a piston: the triceps at the back and biceps on the front, the three-headed and two-headed dragons of labor. The muscles wind toward the shoulder, anchoring their five heads in and around the bones. Their origin lies just below the watchful eye of a raven who perches on the bony outcrop at the crest of my shoulder called the coracoid process: *coraco* is Greek for *raven*.

The wing of the raven sweeps back along the ridge of my shoulder and shapes the escarpment of muscle above my clavicle, so named because it resembles an ancient key or locking bolt. The clavicle is one of the keys that unlocks the vault of the body's wisdom; the left clavicle opens the heart. Where humans have two separate clavicles connected across the top of the sternum, birds have one continuous collarbone called the wishbone, or furculum, which means "merry thought."

The contour of my shoulder descends in an arc toward my back, where the large, thin trapezius muscle wraps and protects the network of muscles behind my heart. It lies across the bulk of both shoulder blades, the scapulae, which are like small wings and whose name is lent to the scapulated raven, *Corvus scapulatus*. The scapulae are also the source of the name for the short shoulder covering called a scapulary – first used by the Benedictines – that monks wear when engaged in physical labor. The entire upper shoulder thus takes the shape of a bird looking skyward as well as that of a laborer intent on the gifts of the earth. Working this part of the body unlocks the heart to soar and frees the hands to shape.

As I work, bending and pressing and listening to the smooth whisper of the shavings as they emerge from the throat of the plane, I imagine the sound to be the warbled notes of the raven perched on my shoulder. I feel it as an aubade traveling up from the ancient bones of this wood; a song of long years of gentle life in the forest, the stillness of falling leaves and of bright, silent winters cocooned in welcoming snow. And of summers of green leaves and a canopy sparkling with light and shadow. My collarbones shift with the work, my chest begins to open, and I feel as though I am myself becoming part of the song.

The trapezius muscle – named for its trapezoidal shape and not, as commonly thought, because it is the muscle one uses to hang on a trapeze or because it looks like a trapeze – assists my arms by bringing in the weight and mass of my back. In conjunction with the latissimus dorsi, which drapes the lower back like a fan (a *lattice*), the trapezius and the many other muscles beneath it allow me to put my back into the work. If I fail to put my back into it enough, I'll end up with a chip on my shoulder, and if that goes on long enough I'll become spineless, and no one will want to back me up. Everyday language is sprinkled with indications of how deeply we understand, at a cultural level, the way the body speaks.

As my hands and arms tire, the maple not yet smooth, I begin to rock back and forth with the rhythm of the plane, pressing forward as the shavings make a trill like a fishing lure sent out on a long cast, looking for the deepest water. The more sustained sound means the shavings are becoming longer, the surface of the wood closer to – but never reaching – absolute flatness. I'm aware of my legs coordinating the motion, the large muscles with names like vastus lateralis and gastrocnemius ("the belly of the leg") pumping to get my trunk on the upswing as I pull the plane back, and rolling down with momentum as I return the plane to the wood. And facilitating it all, way down in the unappreciated hinterland of my body, are my feet. They don't get much fanfare yet make possible many aspects of this work that would otherwise be difficult. Especially the big toe, which in ancient times was called the hallux, meaning "thumb of man": it helps me stay on balance, remain planted firmly in the work. Thus the feet and the hands are companions in the labor of the body, ensuring that I am both solidly grounded and free to glide on the shimmering wings of creative work.

The vault of the body does not always open to the inquiry of work. Sometimes I become distracted, or fickle, or too bent on perfection, and the protean movements that my frame offers me slide into frustrating repetitions of strain or injury or – this is the worst – complete stalling, so that I am left standing sweaty and baffled in the shop, not sure what to do, caught in visions of what's possible but sensing it slip away, birdsong dwindling into the twilight, my muscles sore on tired and fruitless bones.

But when I get it right, when the smallest tremor telegraphed to my fingers by the undulating surface of the wood climbs up into my wrist and forearm, washes my shoulder with the widening sensation of something about to be revealed, when the motion of my back feels like the earth swinging in its orbit — during those moments my heart rises like a raven bursting from the forest floor, rushing up through the canopy and spreading burnished wings to the clear and infinite day.

Amid all the activity of those moments, my hands guiding the tool as it reveals the emerging face of the wood, emotion thrumming through me in bright sparks of feeling, I am always held by an inner stillness — within the flurry of flapping wings, through the rhythm of my muscles as they follow their concise paths, beneath the vault of my heart with its chambers of memory. The ancient Taoists called this state of internal quietude a living midnight in which the golden blossoms of our original essence shine like stars.

The small maple workpiece is done. Waves of grain the color of raw silk sweep across the bright surface of the wood. Despite its somewhat pedestrian reputation, maple is among the world's most versatile woods. The eastern white maple and rock maple varieties used in cabinet-making and furniture are exceedingly strong without being too heavy, offer straight grain, and can be shaped well with hand tools. In Britain, maple lintels and doorsteps were once thought to ward off witches and protect against lightning. This seems relevant to the project at hand, for nothing so disturbs the work of stillness as a bolt of lightning. And I need that stillness, that inner quietude, to assist me in making a small wooden plane.

More than any other woodworking tools, planes are the emissaries of stillness. The rhythmic motion, the murmur of the wood, the slow and steady refinement the steel presses upon it – these things contribute to the state into which my little block plane so faithfully delivers me. I cherish my block plane, yet I have the impulse to build another that is slighter larger, a plane fashioned by my own hands, an emissary of my own making.

The ability to make one's own tools is a timeless milestone in woodcraft, the point at which an apprentice becomes a craftsman. My apprenticeship has been under the tutelage of invisible forces, of creative energies that seize me in the most obnoxious and inconvenient ways. My experience with the marimba was a perfect example – who wants to spend the winter in an unheated shop, wrestling with unsolvable riddles, thrashing about as indecipherable music flees into the night? Yet the imperative to work was there, as it often is, prodding me toward a specific form even if the practicality of the piece is questionable. I have to trust that such imperatives serve a larger purpose. At the same time I dread the day when those invisible forces will ask me to make a ship, or a whimsical house in some windswept place.

In learning this craft I am what is usually called self-taught. Yet I don't think of it that way, of my self as the guide, but rather as having learned under the auspices of an elusive presence: the still, implacable mountain of the creative. It makes sense to me that Fu Xi, the most ancient of Taoist sages and the traditionally acknowledged originator of the eight trigrams, is depicted as a living mountain. After all, mountains are symbols of ascent toward refinement, illumination, understanding. They are the abodes of gods and are sometimes gods themselves.

The Taoist trigram for mountain represents the character of the heights: a single solid line – yang – direct and strong, placed above two dashed lines – double yin. The shape of the yin lines creates an open space in the middle of the trigram, as though a still, calm center waits to be discovered. "Empty yourself of everything," asserts Lao Tzu:

> Let the mind rest at peace.
> The ten thousand things rise and fall while the
> Self watches their return.
> They grow and flourish and then return to the
> source.

Returning to the source is stillness, which is the way of nature.

Making a wooden plane begins with selecting a block of hard and stable wood such as maple and cutting it into three segments to fashion the plane's body: two cheeks and a center block to house the blade. I've just finished planing off the saw marks from those cuts and now have the basic segments roughed out. The sole will come later, after the body has been completed. (This sounds like a bit of Taoist alchemy: *The soul will come when the body is complete.*)

Once the cheeks are shaped and smoothed, I must cut the center block with a wide V into two segments: the front ramp, where shavings will collect, and the rear ramp, where the blade will rest. The rear ramp should be positioned in such a way that the blade protrudes through the sole of the plane slightly forward of the middle. The blade acts like a small pivot in determining the movement of the plane, so its placement is important.

The angle of the V-cut for the ramps is important, too. The front ramp must be shallow enough to allow plenty of room for shavings to accumulate and for my fingers to scoop them out. The rear ramp must position the blade in such a way that it has enough leverage to shear off wood fibers. This is a delicate balance, and it's one of the things woodworkers debate endlessly. The

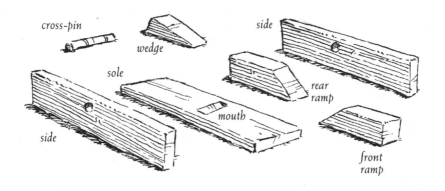

cross-pin

wedge

side

sole

rear
ramp

mouth

side

front
ramp

*The various pieces of a wooden block plane. One traditional meaning of the
word* plane *is "to soar with the wings extended and motionless."*

mechanics involved are complex; since I don't understand them, it seems best just to press on.

I choose an angle of forty-five degrees for the ramps,
smack in the middle between zero and ninety on the
complex spectrum of blade mechanics.[5] I make the cut,
which frees a triangular section and leaves the front and
rear ramps. I save the triangular piece – I'll use it later for
the wedge that will hold the blade in place.

I use a router to shape the cap screw channel. The
cap screw is part of the chip breaker assembly, which
fastens to the blade, stabilizing it and preventing shavings
from growing too large and unwieldy. It is the blade's
companion, the way a scabbard is a sword's companion.
As I shape the channel, the router's spinning cutter sends

small shards of wood out in all directions, like strands of pale confetti or a fireworks of tiny shavings. Then I make the cross-pin, a small wooden bolt like a clavicle designed to hold the wedge and blade in place. I like to make small pieces using only hand tools – knives, rasps, rifflers – so I spend a quiet hour just whittling, shaping the pin and test-fitting it, trying not to slice the ends of my fingers. I pay attention to the way my hands hold the wood, search for where it's still rough, slide over the smooth parts where the work is done.

Now, with all the parts of the body complete (but not the sole), I'm ready to assemble the plane with glue. I place the cross-pin through its mounting holes and position the cheeks on either side of the ramps that will house the open throat. As I go through the steps of naming and placing each piece, I realize how much their names – throat, cheeks, mouth – evoke the language of the voice, of singing. This feels good and right for the use to which this instrument will be put.

When the glue is dry, I unclamp the pieces and inspect the finished plane body. The joints are tight and clean. Now for the sole, which I'll fashion from lignum vitae, the "wood of life," hardest of all woods. Its interlocking grain creates an incredibly tough network of wood fibers lubricated by natural oils that reduce sliding friction. In the West Indies, Colombia, and Venezuela, lignum vitae has traditionally been thought to possess healing powers;

in woodworking its hardness and lubricity make it the best choice for the soles of planes.

I cut the sole to size on the bandsaw, taking care not to blunt the edge of the blade with such dense material. Then, using concealed pegs and epoxy glue – both will increase the bond of the sole to the body – I clamp the pieces firmly and leave them to dry overnight. I can sense my enthusiasm growing. I'm approaching the point at which these various carefully shaped parts will suddenly awaken into their own quiet life.

With the sole affixed I make final adjustments to the mouth of the plane, where shavings will spiral up toward the throat. Technically, the mouth is the opening in the sole through which the blade protrudes like a sharp tongue. The throat is where the shavings end up, farther up the body of the plane alongside the cheeks. The mouth must be formed precisely: wide enough that the blade can move through it in a range of depths, yet narrow enough that it holds the surface of the wood flat just in front of the blade. When the mouth is properly formed, wood fibers are pressed down right up to the moment they encounter the blade. This helps prevent "tearout" of the wood. The term is self-descriptive but doesn't begin to capture the frustration one experiences when chunks of the wood suddenly tear off, leaving ragged cavities in an otherwise smooth surface. I pay close attention to the mouth, using my sharpest and favorite chisel – forged of

Japanese *aogami hagane,* or fine "blue steel" – to pare away the excess wood in small increments, feeling the hard lignum vitae yield to the steel. The final strokes of the chisel are a joy: simple, rewarding work.

I fit the blade into the throat as though the plane were swallowing a sword. Then I shape the small maple wedge that will press against the cross-pin and hold the blade in place during use. This takes a bit of finicking, pushing the blade into place, carefully inserting the wedge, looking for gaps in the mating surface or signs of poor alignment. But in the end it fits; the entire assembly is solid and strong. The last thing now – the very last – is flattening the sole.

Among the several factors that determine the quality of a plane – smoothness and stability of the blade housing, trueness of the various parts, comfort in the hand, quality of the steel – none is more important than the flatness and durability of the sole. It must be superbly flat to smooth other wood surfaces. It is like the human soul in this way: its highest nature is to be still, level, the surface of an undisturbed pool reflecting an endless sky.

The soles of almost all modern planes are made of steel stamped out in factories, where the tolerances are generous. The work of final flattening is usually left to the craftsman. The most effective way to flatten a sole is first to find a dead level surface; the table on a jointer or a good quality tablesaw will do, though plate glass is the best choice. The next step is to glue down fine abrasive paper or apply a slurry of abrasive particles and press the sole against the liquid surface until no bumps or hollows are visible. Working in this way, one begins to see that factory steel is rough indeed, that it is possible to flatten a plane sole so thoroughly the steel begins to shine with its own calm light that is indeed like a quiet pool.

The traditional Taoists have their own ideas about flattening the soul, preparing it for proper use: alchemical practices, esoteric spiritual exercises, mysterious philosophies. These devotions are intended to provide a means of refining the spirit, of flattening out the self-important ego, of letting go of illusion. They call this work, among other things, "cooking in the cauldron of the eight trigrams."[6] It is a means of transformation, as the wood in my hands is being transformed, and as I am being transformed by the work of my hands.

I move the sole back and forth on the surface of the glass, wet and dark with abrasive particles. I gaze into its surface, watching, waiting for the image to clear. And when it does, I'll see my own true face, what the ancient Taoists would call my original face. But I don't see that face, at least not yet. Instead, I see a mountain.

From the back patio of our little house in Maui on the slope where Pu'u Kukui, the "hill of enlightenment," meets the sea, I could trace with my eye the path we had chosen to climb. The long, knife-edge ridge was clearly visible as it rose up from the lowlands, growing more dense as it went until it disappeared into a canopy spread out across a stretch of terrain, deep in shadow, that lay beneath the summit. The grove of pines on the peak made a small outline against the backdrop of the brightening day. Along the remote, lush slopes of Pu'u Kukui, the most pristine spirit of nature still prevailed: stars wheeling overhead and the earth, replete, humming.

There were about a dozen of us, but it was as if I made the trip alone. From the moment we stepped into the shade of the trail, damp and red with the mud of Maui, I went deeply into myself, into the spirit of that place, and remained under its spell. We followed the trail we had been told about, the one we thought had been made by wild boars. It was clear only at ground level, a beaten, earthen track crisscrossed by an infinite web of roots. At knee level it gave way to the dense branches of over-hanging trees and vines. Though I could follow the trail without difficulty, my legs and torso were consistently pressed and scraped by sharp branches indignant at the intrusion. The network of bloody scratches along my body grew as we climbed higher. It was like being tattooed by the rain forest.

Perhaps it was not boars that made the path. It could as easily have been the *menehune*, elves of Hawaiian lore who live deep in the mountains and are renowned as craftsmen.

Or other elusive beings: after all, Taoist legend speaks of Peng-lai, the island abode of immortals, somewhere in the sea east of China. Ancient explorers seeking the sacred mushrooms of that place claim to have seen the island vanish into the depths.[7] Maui lies directly east of China, at a distance of about 5,000 miles; and I have seen the low clouds of an approaching tropical storm hide even the high peaks of that island behind great bastions of moisture that reflect the sea and erase the land, giving the impression of a dark blue sky that extends to the horizon.

The trail climbed toward the shoulder of the mountain. As we made our way farther into the rain forest, the air was brushed with scarlet wings as small birds fed on the nectar of flowers, their petals bright splashes of color. The sounds of our journey were dampened by the abundance of soft green moss, fed by four hundred inches of rainfall each year, that grew on every exposed surface. The day was still. I was aware of my feet on the trail, my hands pushing aside the swinging branches, the sharp sensation of another scratch when I failed to catch one in time — yet beneath these more immediate sensations I began to feel the mountain: listening, watching, waiting.

We climbed for roughly three hours along a narrow ridge. As the trail ascended, the ground fell away on either side until, high up, the path became a narrow passage along a sharp crest with hundreds of feet of vertical drop on either side. On the cliffs a riot of climbing shoots, creepers, and moss filled every niche. Shrubs and hardy trees clung to the face, their branches and trunks meandering out into empty air and back again. Eventually the crest opened out onto a wider, more gentle slope from which we could see down into Honokohau Valley with its sheer, thousand-foot cliff of many waterfalls called "the wall of tears." Farther on we stopped for a rest at Violet Lake, where a rare form of native violet nestled alongside greensword, lobelia, and tiny ohia with their soft-spiked red blossoms.

The bright day gave way to clouds and mist on the mountain's upper reaches. We climbed higher, no longer able to see the summit but following the rough trail through shadows. I was not aware of time, but moved through the territory as though I had always walked there, a traveler drifting through the landscape like a breath in the damp air.

The afternoon must have worn on, because at some point we stopped and made the decision to turn back before reaching the summit. We had come to an open bog that lay beneath the peak itself, and there was some risk that if we did not begin the return journey soon we might find ourselves on the lower trail during nightfall. With this in mind the group gathered together for a short snack before retreating from the mountain's slopes.

I was glad we stopped, for as I had climbed higher it became clear to me that the summit was a place of ancient sacredness. It would have seemed an intrusion, a trespass, to enter that domain without a specific and compelling purpose. We had none. A small grove of trees lay to one side of the bog and I wandered over there. I wanted to be alone in this most remote place, to sit and listen to water dripping on the leaves. But I never quite formed those thoughts. Rather I found myself, at a certain moment, within a rough circle made by the moss-covered trees. Looking up through the branches overhead, I could see clouds, dark in the dwindling day.

I stayed in the grove for some time, soaking up the stillness, becoming aware of something primordial within me – a wind blowing from a distant threshold, its breath on my neck the most ephemeral touch. I stood motionless among the trees. I became so still I forgot who I was. Or perhaps I remembered myself, saw my own true face. It's hard to say, even now. Nothing moved, and yet the grove was saturated with bursting life. Time slowed, and stopped. There was no time. No *I*.

And then, distantly, I heard a sound – no, not just a sound, a name. Someone was searching, calling, and as I heard the sound of the name spread itself out across the landscape, I began to ask myself if that name belonged to me. Aeons passed while I pondered this question. And then I decided it must be mine – no one else seemed to be claiming it – and I slowly came out from under the spell of that stillness. I turned and saw one of our party on a nearby slope, his hands cupped around his mouth, calling me back. So often have I been called back. I looked toward the grove one last time and then turned away, toward the sound of my name.

According to the Hawaiian creation story, the Kumulipo, which means "deep source," or "source from within the darkness," a woman named La'ila'i was born during the time of the earth's first ages, the time of gods and the oldest of creatures. Her name means *stillness*, calmness. She lived among "the first chiefs of the dim past dwelling in cold uplands." As we traveled back down the trail toward the shore, toward the bright sun of the beach, I wondered if such ancient beings might still inhabit the high places of these islands.

The plate glass beneath the sole of the plane now seems deep with memory. As I've been pressing down, moving the plane in a figure eight across the surface, the sole has flattened and begun to swirl the abrasive in sinuous waves and eddies of dark motion. I know I'm done when the slurry moves on the glass without disturbances or irregularities. The wood of the sole and the surface of the glass are perfectly mated. The glass is a still pool.

I remove the plane from the glass and dry off the sole, taking care to change cloths several times until smudges from the wet abrasive no longer appear on the fabric. The feeling of the high and ancient grove of Pu'u Kukui stays with me as I finish the plane, as I shape the sides and back with a rasp and file, as I fit the body to my hand with its creases and lines. I work in silence, not thinking about the result, just working. I lose track of time.

Eventually I see that the plane is finished. I sharpen the blade — dark streaks of swarf trace the edges of my fingers — insert it into the mouth, select a piece of straight pine from the offcut bin and gently rest the plane on the wood. I push it tentatively, feeling its shape with my fingers, noticing the muscles in my arms and shoulders, sensing the raven, perched beside my ear, whispering messages sent from the Hawaiian god Maui, whose shape is a hawk. Maui is famous for having fished up the North Island of New Zealand from the bottom of the sea using a hook made from his grandmother's jawbone and blood from his own nose as bait. What is less known is that Maui's hook first snagged not on submerged land but on the porch of a carved wooden house. Wood is often at the beginning of things. And, as with Sadie's box, at the end of things, too.

A thin shaving spirals up with a gentle susurrus from the mouth of the plane. It works — of course it works, why do I doubt my craft? My body responds with a joyous shiver, my clavicles opening all the secret vaults of my heart, my back wide with accomplishment, my legs strong and solid. Even my feet are happy.

I make shavings. Buckets of shavings. Enough shavings to fill my sawdust bin. Long, thin ribbons of wood

dance out of the plane with a song that grows more vig-
orous as I work. I'm not working toward anything, not
making anything; just planing, soaring. And in the midst
of all this activity – the shavings, my body with its rhythm,
the bright day new and new again – I grow still inside, a
place of ancient and secret beginnings.

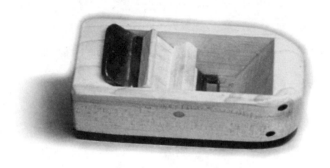

## 6

# S H A L L O W S

THIS ROWBOAT IS OLD, WORN DOWN SO thoroughly by memories and by the sea that it seems, resting atop two sawhorses in my shop, almost insubstantial. The overturned hull is faded and chalky, crackled with scars. The central seat (the thwart) has been worn away where it joins the fiberglass and now rests crookedly against the hull. The transom seat is splintered and worn. Gaps left by missing planks expose the buoyancy foam beneath, pocked with age and sodden from forty years of damp. The bow seat is fractured and rickety; the screws anchoring it are corroded enough to look like fat nails. When I tug on the seat, feeling for how securely it might be fastened, it breaks loose from the hull with a cascade of rotted wood and crumbling foam. Useless. Yet I remember when my younger brother was four or five and he would curl himself up in this small nook at the bow, his body folded beneath the gunwale, his head poking up and forward into the breeze. The boat was almost new at that time, fresh, unshadowed by the derelict before me.

The gunwales are cracked almost along their entire length. Scores of holes drilled in them for repair or adding hardware or who-knows-what forgotten scheme have widened with decay into rows of ragged, black-stained tears in the hull. And the hull itself is in poor shape indeed: deep scratches cut through the paint virtually everywhere below the waterline, white traces of undercoat press through the faded orange surface. Alongside the battered keel the paint has been almost completely scraped away. I run my hand over the damaged surface, wondering if the fiberglass beneath is cracked. As a child I stood in this boat on countless rocky shores, watching the hull flex under pressure from the stones beneath. It would not surprise me at all to find internal damage within this aged skin.

Wandering from one catastrophe to the next, poking around this old hulk that is no longer seaworthy, I am daunted by the task of restoring it. Yet that's the plan — to make this craft anew, reclaim for it a place on the water. It feels good that I will also be reawakening my memory of this fragile boat as I work, revisiting those summers so long ago. Each disintegrating part speaks its own history. Here, along the outside curve of the bow, is where we ran into the fishboat on that sunny afternoon in Georgia Strait, the heat of the day and swell of the sea rocking us into such thorough relaxation that no one noticed the craft in our path until it was too late. The long crack in the fiberglass is still there, hidden beneath the gunwale. Along the stern I find the twin impressions left by the clamping screws of our three-horsepower Evinrude motor. They remind me of the scar on my leg from the time I swam too close to the spinning propeller. And I remember fastening the folding motor on, pulling the starter cord, jamming the white throttle lever all the way to its stop and holding on to the seat as the bow shot into the air. I'd clamber forward, bring the bow down with my weight and sit in the bow seat, steering the boat by leaning from side to side, using the curve of the hull like a paddle slicing through the water.

Here, look, the screw holes from the old traveler — where has all that old sailing gear gone, anyway? Probably squirreled away at my dad's place alongside ancient, rotting sails and windsurfing hardware collected over the years from half a dozen boards. The remains of the old sailing hardware still on the boat, a crumbling wreckage of brass and steel and corroded screws – it all has to come off. Right down to the shell. It's pretty clear this won't be an act of restoration as much as a complete rebuilding from the stripped hull. Even that may need extensive work, and I suppose it might be more efficient simply to build a new boat. But then I'd lose more than I hope to gain here.

The gunwales come off first. The threads of the countersunk bronze bolts that fasten them to the hull are corroded beyond use, so I slice through the metal with a cutoff blade in my jigsaw. The segments fall to the floor with the brittle, snapping sound of wood bleached of its natural oils and further degraded by years of exposure to salt air. The smell of rot, sharp and damp, spreads out across the shop.

I remove the remnants of the bow seat and thwart, twisting out the old fasteners with a pair of locking pliers. The heads of the screws are a mess of corrosion. The transom seat is fastened more securely, its buoyancy foam still intact enough to provide a solid base. I bang the slats free with a hammer and rip out the old foam with a sturdy scraper, separating it from the hull with long sweeps of the tool. The foam cracks off in great chunks and falls away with a frail, shivery sound.

A small brass plaque fastened with nails at each corner lies just above the transom seat. The inscription, now white with oxidation, reads:

DAVIDSON MFG. CO. LTD.
1872 WEST GEORGIA ST.
VANCOUVER, B.C.
SERIAL   5973

Hamish Davidson was one of the original fiberglass boatbuilders in Canada, setting up shop in the early thirties down by Stanley Park (the site is now home to one of the most upscale apartment buildings in the country). He started out as a maker of wooden skis; my dad remembers buying a pair when he was sixteen. Davidson then began building laminated wooden boats and in 1949 started using fiberglass over the wood. Pretty soon all the boats were made of fiberglass; a natural shift, as fiberglass is far superior to wood for marine structural applications. Not as traditional or crafty as wood, but fiberglass is lighter, stronger, can be made flexible or rigid, is easier to work, and is less expensive. Sure, wood looks better – a finely fitted teak deck is a tapestry of beautiful grain – but fiberglass won't rot, and that makes it hard to beat. Besides, the traditional boatbuilding woods such as teak, mahogany, and greenheart have been overharvested almost to the point of extinction. It's hard to believe that teak, perhaps the greatest and most versatile of woods, is on its way to vanishing from the world. Or perhaps it's not so hard to believe.

Davidson made thousands of small boats over the years. Our little craft, a D9 put together in 1959, was almost six thousand boats along that manufacturing line. The D9 model was popular as a dinghy and day sailer; small fleets of them used to race around Coal Harbor. But during the seventies, after Hamish had retired and his son took over, things got tougher and eventually the company foundered. Nowadays there's nothing left of Davidson Manufacturing except the old dinghies that still make their battered way through these waters.

I remove the keel strip that runs along the inside centerline of the hull in preparation for removing the keel. The strip is so worn that bits of it have virtually dissolved, revealing the thin fiberglass beneath. This is where leaks would have penetrated the hull, where the keel fasteners pass through the fiberglass. I can see the rubbery evidence of many failed repair attempts with silicone. On a hull such as this, formed as one continuous shape in a fiberglass mold, fastener holes present the only vulnerability to leakage. Boatbuilders take great pains to seal the holes with silicone or polyester resin, but eventually, inevitably, the fasteners work loose over time as the hull is twisted and rolled through the water. Even on a large sailboat the keel fasteners must be tightened periodically.

If a keel is sealed properly, the fasteners can loosen just a bit inside the keel housing without allowing water to enter, but since the keel on this boat is made of wood, and wood degrades, water has found its way in.

As I extract the keel strip fasteners near the bow, I discover a particularly large glop of silicone plugging a hole where the old bow eye came loose. A new hole has been drilled through the hull just above the old one; the stainless steel of the bow eye is bright where the bowline passes through the smooth ring. It's the only piece of serviceable gear left on the boat. This makes sense. After all, a bow eye is pretty much the only gear you need on a dinghy other than oarlocks. All that towing around, the dinghy riding quietly at the stern, unobtrusive, sliding over thousands of miles of water, held to its course by a single bow eye with a shank of quarter-inch steel.

When we were kids, my brothers and I used to climb into this dinghy and pay out a long rope behind our parents' sailboat. We'd sit in there for hours, tethered by the bow eye, my younger brother up front, my older brother in the stern, and me on the thwart. We'd lean our weight to one side and then the other, swinging the dinghy back and forth on its tether, seeing how far we could get it to shoot out to one side before being jerked back by the painter. We'd drag our hands in the water, splash each other, see who was strong enough to grab the rope and pull us forward along our line of travel. And

when we came to a new cove or harbor or landing, we'd
cast off in the dinghy to explore, rowing it through tidal
pools and across shallow reaches called tombolos that
became mud flats at low tide; if you were quick enough,
you could sometimes pull up a geoduck.

We rowed this small craft around countless tiny islands
of the Inside Passage, eased it into sheltered bays where
seals popped up to take a look. Sometimes the sleek, black
fin of an orca crested the distant surface of the water. And
when we'd had enough of exploring, we'd take the dinghy
out and capsize it, rolling it over and over again as we
swam underneath to find the air pocket, clambered on
top to escape the cold water, sputtered and whooped with
the simple, sustaining joy of being wholly alive. Now,
with fragments of the gunwales and seats and keel strip
scattered on the floor beside the derelict hull, that aliveness seems remote from the craft before me.

I inspect the seam carefully where the keel and hull
meet. I'm not sure what measures were taken, in addi-
tion to fasteners, to hold the keel in place. Silicone sealant
and marine glue were likely used, so removing the fasteners is only half the job. I place my hand on the keel
at the stern, at its widest point, and rock it back and forth,
feeling for play. There's a shudder of movement, but it's
nowhere near being loose. Usually, joints secured with
glue or old silicone sealant have a fairly low tolerance for
movement and shear loose in response to persistent

wiggling. But here there's nothing. I don't want to tear
it off; I like to think of myself as a gentle craftsman sensitive enough to coax things gently apart. I'm also aware
that this self-perception is a romantic illusion, an appeal
to old-world sensibilities. Fact is, I have a really big
framing hammer for such contingencies. I fetch it from
the toolbox, take careful aim so as not to hit the fiberglass,
and strike the keel with a resounding whack. The entire
rear segment flies off, three feet of rotting teak cart-
wheeling across the shop. So much for delicate sensibilities. It's no use tapping lightly away in these kinds of
situations: that's likely to stretch and tear things even
more. You're better off with a quick, strong stroke that
goes for maximum shearing action. Sometimes it works.
Sometimes it makes things worse.

In his discussion of the roots of art, Lewis Hyde
emphasizes the role of the trickster, the mythological
emissary of joyful, irreverent spontaneity. Hyde draws a
parallel between the trickster's creative process and the
act of joining, or disjointing, of articulating or redraw-
ing the meaningful connections between things (why is
a raven like a writing desk?). The trickster's role, he asserts,
is to articulate and rework the joints, the hinges where
different realities meet. Thus the terms *art* and *articulate*
(as in the articulated joints of the body as well as the
magic of speech) derive from the same root, *artus*. In
speaking of the evolution of creative intention in the

trickster, Hyde confirms that "attacking the joints to actually destroy something, or attacking the joints so as to
change the shape of things: these are the first two senses
in which tricksters are *artus*-workers and their creations
works of *artus*."[8]

I bang loose the remaining keel segments, jarring each
one free with a percussive wallop. The fiberglass beneath
the keel is undamaged, its surface sealed by the wood all
this time. Bits of polyester resin on the flat, inside surface
of the keel show where the joint was glued down.

I retrieve the scattered segments of the keel and return
the hammer. It's good to work on a reasonably simple
project, not too finicky, the kind of thing where I'm not
haunted by a constant dread of making one final, fatal
slip that wrecks it all. With this old craft and my many
memories, with the relative simplicity of these tasks and
the feeling of restoring what would otherwise have been
lost, a nascent mood begins to flower: lighter, more
relaxed. Not so much at stake. Joyfulness is a creative
energy associated by the Taoists with lakes, rivers, and
other shallow bodies of water. Whereas deep water pulls
downward, draws me into elemental and transformative
dreams – black, dark dreams, some of them – the shallows
are a realm of playfulness and fluidity, drawing me along
silver, sparkling paths of moving water. "Tao in the world
is like a river flowing home to the sea," as the Taoists say.
Joyfulness in creative work can be a path leading home.

Yet it's not that straightforward. I seldom slip into a blissful zone where I forget my troubles, where the essential creative flow fills me up, replete and whole. Sometimes I get a few moments of that, mostly when I'm planing wood. The struggles I hold on to most tightly do fall away in those moments and I am freed, briefly, to wander through an experience of the simple, of the real. But I spend quite a bit more time in this craft swearing and injuring my fingers and worrying about how it's all going to turn out. I complain about the materials and the process and my lack of skill. I grow impatient, make careless mistakes out of frustration, forget to follow simple steps, and set myself back in many ways.

Yet somehow, through these twists and turns in which I try to fit myself into the work in a way that also fits me, I do find a rich joyfulness. It arises from the feeling of being shaped by unseen hands, flows out of the sense that I am being crafted by creative forces that answer to many names. That's why I get injured, why I am cajoled and prodded by the work: I'm being abraded and worn down and made true. There's a joyful discovery in that circular or spiral relationship between the maker and the made.

I might as well get the toughest part out of the way first: refinishing the hull. All the old finish has to come off, right down to the fiberglass, down past the deepest scratches to where I can start to build it up again. It takes two dedicated days while the kids and Elizabeth are away, enough toxic chemicals to poison every cat in the neighborhood, and my belt sander working so hard that the motor housing burns my hand when I touch it in a careless moment. Dust. Fumes. Sweat.

I work my way around the hull from bow to stern, scraping and sanding through the faded orange topcoat, discovering the brown fairing compound beneath, pushing through to the white primer coats and finally coming upon the original gelcoat finish applied in the fiberglass mold: a deep, sunset orange. When that, too, is removed and the raw, scratched fiberglass hull begins to emerge in the driveway, I come round to the stern to finish it off and find, buried by two generations of accumulated paint and time and memory, the black letters that had been painted over so long ago and that are now barely legible. Hand-painted in chunky, square letters in the days before anyone knew what a font was, the original name of this dinghy appears: *Cookie Monster*.

I leave the last layers of paint on the stern for a few days while I work on other parts of the hull, straying back every so often to run my fingers across the old letters, still remembering the night when our family gathered together at the kitchen table and settled on that name.

I work for two weeks toward a smooth hull: sanding, fairing, inspecting, fairing again, sanding again. Power sanding and wet sanding, filling smaller and smaller imperfections with polyester compound. It gives off such a powerful solvent smell that a single whiff sends me wandering aimlessly around the shop, fiddling with piles of sawdust, spacey enough to lose focus entirely.

The work progresses. The fiberglass grows more smooth and clear and I begin to see into the layers that make up the hull. The view is not good. Throughout the central section of the hull, where the forest of scratches was deepest, the fiberglass has been twisted beyond its capacity. Deep torsion cracks trace their way through the woven structure. Most are internal shears, but in one spot the crack goes all the way through. I hadn't counted on this – it doubles the work I'll have to do. Frustrating. But I'm feeling patient about the work, trusting in its rhythm. The moment passes and I settle once again into this resonant, remembering work.

When I was a boy I spent summers on the Sunshine Coast, north of Vancouver, at my grandmother's summer place. I slept downstairs, at ground level, in a room that faced east with a window overlooking the beach. Sometimes I'd be awakened in the early morning by the rising sun extending a long fiery finger across the water. I'd climb out of bed, open the patio door and amble down to the beach, where logs that had drifted in perhaps a century ago offered a warm and quiet place to sit. I'd think about my father coming here when he was a boy, watching gulls glide on the morning breeze, waiting for the first ferry to swing around the point into view. Sometimes there'd be a boat out early, a group of water-skiers or a trawler heading for the gap into the Strait. Its bow would part the silken waters as though the first story of the world were unfolding. The sun would sparkle on the wake, the craft would glide through the first moments, before words and night and time, when the circling seagull and the pebbles onshore knew each other's names in an unspoken and elemental language. Often, as I waited on the shore, I listened for the words of that secret language played out by the rhythm of the waves, the warmth of the sun, the breeze rattling the hedge beside the house. And in those unfolding moments my sense of my father's boyhood would merge with my own and I would almost lose track of my distinctiveness, sliding into place like a pearl on its string, threaded into a long strand of moments, each one the first.

There are two ways to repair torsion cracks within a fiberglass hull: from the inside or from the outside. In this way hulls are somewhat like human beings. I can either apply a new layer of fiberglass cloth over the hull's damaged exterior, redoing all that work of fairing and filling – or I can glass the inside, where the finished surface need not be absolutely smooth. I've done quite a bit of work already, smoothing the hull, readying it for a new finish, and I have no intention of working backwards now that my efforts have revealed the deeper cracks. I'll finish the exterior hull first and then turn the boat over to work on the inside.

On a warm day in the first week of June, I apply a coat of thick fiberglass primer to the exterior hull. It's about the consistency of whipping cream and dries almost as soon as I put it on. I work frantically, splattering the stuff on my shorts, spilling it on the driveway, trying to make sure I've covered the surface adequately before it sets up. I wear a respirator to protect me from the strong smell of xylene used in the primer as a thinning agent. It's a particularly nasty solvent to which, over the years, I've developed a sensitivity. One whiff of the stuff and my brain starts to cramp. The respirator works quite well, with its twin filtering canisters sticking out on either side of my face, but every time I wince at another little spill or coax myself on, mumbling imprecations into the mask, the movements of my face lift the rubber seal around my nose and mouth and a tiny puff of xylene sneaks in. It has a peculiar scent, as though apples and iron had been mixed together in a tincture of battery acid.

When the primer is dry, I wash the hull down and go to work with wet/dry sandpaper, smoothing out the white surface, which is now uniform enough that I can see all the tiny imperfections I missed on the mottled, bare fiberglass. Then another coat of primer goes on, another flurry of rushing and slopping and fretting. One more round of sanding and I'm ready for the paint.

Elizabeth chooses a deep, Cookie Monster blue. The label on the can grandly calls it sapphire blue, as though the boat will be a jewel. The paint is designed to be applied with spray equipment, and I've always had poor luck with sprayers. I tend to slather it on, creating runs and pools along edges and in corners. Usually I try to even out the flow by applying even more paint, which eventually results in a glutinous, inchoate mess. In any craft there are things one learns to avoid, techniques and methods for which no amount of practice leads any closer to proficiency. It's best to have a fallback strategy.

There is a trick to applying marine paint with a roller and brush. I roll it on in wide strips from the gunwale to the keel and then use a fine, dry bristle brush to tip off the bubbles left by the roller. I draw the brush gently across the paint, not applying any pressure, working from bow to stern. In this way it is possible to create a hand-applied finish that has the characteristic sheen of a sprayed surface. That's what I'm going for. Over the next several days I apply four coats to the hull in my driveway, wincing and swearing every time a bit of pollen drifts down from the trees onto the wet paint.

I'm out in my paint-stained shorts and shirt, waving at the neighbors, keeping an eye out so the kids don't run into the street, cursing the pollen while I apply a finish that I want to be a sheet of conformity, completely void of individual uniqueness. Not exactly a model of creative genius. I'm just a workaday guy trying to give his kids a chance to feel wind on water on a sunny afternoon. Yet creative energy is everywhere here: in my mood, in my craft, in the way the damned pollen finds the smoothest and most perfected spots to land, even in the funny, indulgent looks I get from the neighbors. That's the thing about creative process; it always lies beyond the reach of definition, can't be stacked up into categories and laid out for view. Creative work tears down those categories and washes all fixed forms downstream like so much silt, leaving only the inescapable river. The *flow*.

Trying to define creative process is like planing without the blade in, or trying to hammer water into a shape — it doesn't get you far. Yet sometimes the water *does* take a shape, something that's a fantastic hybrid between your own craft and the unpredictable magic of manifestation. A crazy philosopher's stone, a jewel of promise and wisdom and becoming. *Jewel*, from the same root as *joy*.

The old European alchemists, who were a great deal like the ancient Taoists, believed the philosopher's stone would integrate opposites, join all the truths into a long, clear thread leading to unity. The joyfulness of creative process, of craft, lies in finding the strands of that unity and hauling on them like kids in a rowboat trying to catch up with the wind. Creative joy is about the articulation of the joints that connect all the worlds: the inner and the outer, the upper and the lower, the false and the true. The *I Ching* says:

> As water provides moisture for myriad beings, joy develops myriad beings; joyful within and without, reaching the outer from within, communicating with the inner from without, inside and outside are conjoined, without separation between them – therefore it is called *joy*.

The outer part of the hull is done. It's time to work on the inner shell, joining the fiberglass throughout and swallowing those torsion cracks up within a larger strength and unity.

Working with wood is an exercise in patience and precision. Many perils arise from the fact that the material is rigid and unforgiving. There's no slack, hardly any room for error. Thus a woodworking adage, a Murphy's Law about the challenge of accuracy, predicts that any piece cut to length will be too short. Wood is a stubborn ally. But working with fiberglass, that's a different universe altogether.

In 1932, the same year that Hamish Davidson began making laminated wooden skis, an American researcher at the Owens-Illinois glass company made a creative mistake, an accidental joining of two worlds. He unintentionally sprayed a jet of compressed air onto a stream of molten glass; the glass stretched itself out under the air's pressure, twisting and whirling into countless shimmering, luminous filaments. This inadvertent discovery, brought to light by what was essentially a dearth of skill in spraying (at least I can point the sprayer in the right direction), led to the development of fiberglass and a subsequent technological revolution.

Fiberglass is composed of two separate materials: woven glass fibers and liquid polyester resin. Mixed together, articulated, the glass and resin make an impressive conjuncture: resilient and substantial and forgiving all at once. If you make a mistake, you just add more, or grind off the offending bit and shape the rest as you like. There's no patient finicking as there is with wood. Just slap on the resin, put the cloth down, and paint over with resin again. No careful working to a precise edge, no fiddling with sharp tools and intractable grain. Mix, apply, and wait. Take a break, play in the sprinkler.

There's a downside, too. After all, the woven glass is completely covered by successive coats of resin and the final surface is just smooth, simple plastic. No grain, no diversity, nothing but function. It is good to have a break from the demands of wood, and fiberglass is great for boat hulls, but I wouldn't want a piece of furniture made from the stuff.

I apply the fiberglass cloth carefully to the inside of the hull, taking care to work out the wrinkles as I roll on a heavy coat of resin. I build up two layers at the most vulnerable points on either side of the keel where the torsion cracks lie. I wait for this initial coating to dry, and then, over the course of a week, during busy mornings with the kids or before heading off to teach in the growing warmth of late spring evenings, I apply six coats of resin. I tint the last four with white pigment to give the inside hull a clean, painted look. Now the entire hull is conjoined, integrated, sapphire blue on the outside and bright white on the inside. As I stand back to look at the evolving shape in my driveway, my hands spotted with blue and white hieroglyphs in some forgotten language, this craft no longer derelict but on its way to some new territory of fruition, I begin to see that perhaps it will be a jewel after all.

Sometimes, late in the summer, when sun and breeze had heated the water enough that it was no longer bracing but simply refreshing, when the long dog days of August rolled through the coast in grand waves of sunshine, sometimes on those days we'd go spinnaker flying. We'd moor the sailboat to a piling or dock, wind to the stern, and loft the spinnaker dead downwind. But instead of anchoring the sail lines to their customary blocks near the cockpit, we'd loosely connect the two bottom corners of the sail with a continuous section of rope that hung down in a wide arc to create a sling. A second rope fed back to the foredeck as a way of controlling the sail and retrieving the sling. One of us, usually my older brother, Bob, the bravest among us, would dive in the water and swim for the sling. In later years the lines Bob drew between bravery and bravado blurred as the deep water of our lives exerted an increasing pull, but in those days my younger brother, Bruce, and I were entranced by Bob's raw courage. He'd hoist himself up into the sling and kick his feet in the water to get the rope positioned just right. On the foredeck one of us would let the guide rope out, slowly releasing the sail into the wind and allowing it to fill with that summer air so warm we could feel the texture of the heat. The sail would rise up, pulling Bob with it, the rope of the sling going taut with his weight and lifting him from the water. It was like a parachute, in reverse. The bright colors of the spinnaker would unfurl all their wrinkles and carry Bob higher – level with the deck, then twenty feet above it. It looked as though the grand apparatus might carry him off to the horizon, to whatever place he dreamed of in his quietest sleep, the way I'd see him dreaming sometimes in the early mornings lying in his berth in the fo'c'sle we shared.

Bob would ride the wind for fifteen or twenty minutes, pulling the sling one way or the other to set up a rocking motion in the air, looking down on the deck and shouting that he was level with the spreaders, allowing himself to become a creature of the air for those few minutes. And then we'd pull on the guide rope, the side of the sail would buckle inward, and he'd descend to the water again. He'd swim back to the boat with a manic grin, clamber up the ladder at the stern, grab a towel off the cockpit rail, and watch the next person have a go. He was only a year and a half older than I, but his movements and easy grace and confidence were heroic in my estimation – he was not *sensitive,* that was the essence of it, he was a true and reckless boy. And in my eyes, in the eyes of a ten-year-old unsure of his place and his ability and already wounded by what life dishes out as though it were fair rations, Bob was an exemplar of strength. It's tempting, now that the years have grown into a long wake and the choices we made in those early times seem to have defined us so much, to look at what came later and see the ways in which my brother's strength and confidence were not always a gift. But these are adult considerations. They have no bearing on those simple moments of joyfulness we all felt as the sail lofted us higher and higher, up into the shimmering sky as though it would never stop, almost as though we would be swallowed by that arching blueness and forever be what those moments made of us.

With the fiberglass work completed, I'm ready for the more complex and rewarding task of building new seats, gunwales, and keel. Teak was used originally for the keel but I've ruled it out because of scarcity. The gunwales were oak, but the tannins in oak react with metal fasteners and moisture to turn wood black, which ı want to avoid. And the seats were made of cedar, which though light and plentiful is too splintery and structurally weak for this application. I'm going for a more steadfast and handcrafted boat than before. My choice of woods reflects that orientation.

On a small dinghy the keel and thwart provide underlying rigidity, whereas the gunwales, which move with the hull as it is twisted through the water, must be tough and flexible. Maple is durable and yet resilient, so it will work well for gunwales. The keel is a more complex matter. It should be made of stiff wood, but since weight is always a consideration on a dinghy, it must also be light. Blackwood, jarrah, and other dense seafaring hardwoods are too heavy for a small vessel such as this. The best choice is something in the conifer family, something with a composite cellular structure that imparts great rigidity to the wood without adding excessive weight. This kind of biological architecture allows redwoods and Douglas firs to grow hundreds of feet tall and to resonate with the distinctive musicality of my marimba.[9] The mechanics of that architecture can be expressed in terms of what wood technologists call the modulus of elasticity, a set of ratios that determines the relationship between density and stiffness. For the keel and seats on a small boat, just about the best elasticity ratios are found in Douglas fir.

With their drying time of roughly two inches of thickness per year, the smaller fir planks from last year's flurry of stacking will be getting close to dry. I amble out to the stack alongside the house, push the metal pins of the moisture meter into the wood, spin the dial up through the numbers, and wait for the light to come on. I pass the lower values, the water content percentages of five to seven ideal for cabinetmaking, and at ten the light comes on. I'm surprised the wood is so dry after such a short time. I check two more spots to verify the readings and then take several boards into the shop. I worried so much about what to do with all this fir; now I have a path, a means to bring some of it once more to life.

Rough-sawn wood is thoroughly unlike wood from the lumberyard. Processed wood is cooked in a kiln to dry it quickly, removing most of the wood's unique color. And in every lumber mill there is an anonymous man called the grader, a craftsman's censor who culls the boards with unruly grain, with too many knots, with twists of excessive ingenuity. He's just a guy enforcing quality control. But the most dazzling and evocative wood — the kind of wood that fails to meet the precise standards of mediocrity — is lost through the grader's devotion. Bypassing the kiln and the grader, shaping straight from the tree, is a subversive smuggling past the watchful eyes of the censor. It's like the trickster Hermes stealing the sacred cattle of Apollo, thieving beauty from beneath the gaze of the gods of order and authority.

Rough-sawn boards have no predetermined dimension, have not been cooked into dullness. They are raw, the color of the deep tree still hidden within them. I select one of the long planks and run it through the planer, slicing off the marks from the bandsaw mill and trueing up the top surface. The smoothed wood is a revelation: hues of ocher and umber and a yellow like pale apricots all mixed together in bands of heartwood and sapwood that flow like a river through the board. Most people think of Douglas fir as junk wood, good enough only for roof trusses and plywood. But most people know only the lumberyard fir. What lies here, its sawdust drifting like motes of luminous honey in the air, is the pristine rain-forest fir: bright, diverse, beautiful.

Without measuring, aware of not being constrained by predimensioned stock, I form a new keel. I use my bandsaw and my little block plane, the maple one I made. I shape the keel by eye, not knowing how long or how thick it is, only that it's a little larger than the old one; and I know that it fits the hull precisely.

As I work I am reminded that in Norway traditional sailing vessels called *faerings* were once built entirely by eye, with only the craftsman's hand to measure the proportions, to articulate the joints. To be in such close relationship to the wood, the tools, to one's own body as an instrument of precision, inspires in me a kind of awe. It causes me to work more slowly.

I lay the keel aside for assembly later and begin work on the seats: transom, thwart, and bow. I take advantage of my cabinetmaking skills to joint the various assemblies. The transom seat, which had been half a dozen tongue-and-groove cedar planks nailed to a frame, becomes a single continuous shape of jointed boards matched for grain orientation and appearance. I fashion the thwart from a single foot-wide board with a band of rippled heartwood in the grain. It's rare to find the full width of heartwood, the deep wood at the center of the tree, and sapwood, the outer rings of growth, together in a single plank of processed lumber. The boards are usually not wide enough to contain both elements. But here, with wood from the entire thickness of the tree available for me to use, I have more flexibility. More play.

In all three seats I incorporate peculiarities of the wood – knots, ribbons of darker texture, eddies in the grain – as a means of increasing that play. Woodworkers generally look for straight, even-grained wood because of its stability. Knots introduce weakness to a board because they have a tendency to pop out or buckle the surrounding wood under strain. Knotty pine and bird's-eye maple (the countless tiny eyes are partially formed knots) are prized for their visual appeal, but usually in woodworking, as in many things, vulnerabilities and quirks are often pushed aside in favor of collective uniformity. Less play.

The swirls and patterns and rough patches where the wood reveals, unequivocally, its true source and nature make the seats shimmer with color and variety. I'm not worried about structural problems with the knots, as the wood will be sealed and finished with epoxy, the same material used to make the wing skins of lighter planes. This hybrid between natural and technological forms will be immensely strong and almost impervious to moisture.

As I fashion the seats, matching them to the hull curve for curve, I practice my woodworking skills in unusual ways. Cabinetmaking is almost always a matter of straight lines; I've grown accustomed to assessing right angles, sighting down planks to find true surfaces. In this sense cabinetmaking is two-dimensional, at least compared with boatbuilding. When all the surfaces are flat, all the angles identical, the work is simpler, more predetermined in the same way dimensioned lumber is predetermined. On a boat there are virtually no right angles, no flat surfaces.

Everything I cut to length seems to be half an inch too short. This was a familiar experience when I started woodworking, before I knew how to see and feel the length of a straight stretch of lumber. It takes me a few tries, cutting and recutting, before I figure out that curves have their own dimensionality, liminality; the right coaxing nudges them across the threshold of awkwardness toward a seamless joining. Curves require more slack, an approach both more forgiving and more exacting.

The shaped seats receive four coats of clear epoxy, sealing the wood and providing a smooth, glossy finish. I then pour expanding buoyancy foam into the bulkheads below the bow and transom seats and fasten the seats. As I sit back on my haunches at the level of the gunwale, waiting for the foam to dry, I realize I am no longer working on a derelict shape worn down by the current of time but on an actual boat, a craft of promise. This dinghy is indeed coming to life again.

In the summer of 1792, off the shore of what is now Point Grey on Vancouver's west side, the explorer George Vancouver met, by chance, two Spanish ships captained by Valdes and Galiano. They chose to collaborate for an excursion northward into territory that no European had ever seen: the winding, uncharted track of territory now known as the Inside Passage.[10] Most of the islands and landmarks they encountered still bear the names of ship's officers: Cape Mudge, Mount Baker, the islands Galiano and Valdes. Wandering roughly a hundred miles north of their meeting place, the ships hove to at the mouth of an inlet flanked by steep mountains on either side. Archibald Menzies,[11] the surgeon and botanist on Vancouver's ship *Discovery,* described the anchorage:

... about a mile & a half to the North East of the Ship there was a beautiful Waterfall which issued from a Lake close behind it & precipitated a wide foaming stream into the Sea over a shelving rocky precipice of about thirty yards high. Its wild romantic appearance aided by its rugged situation & the gloomy forests which surrounded it, rendered it a place of resort for small parties to visit during our stay.

This diverse landscape later came to be called Teakerne Arm; it was my favorite of the places we visited on the coast each summer. It lies just north of the area Captain Vancouver described, in a fit of depression at finding so few native inhabitants along the coast, as "desolate." The environment in and around Desolation Sound is odd, paradoxical. Whales and eagles and sea lions populate these waters, plying deep fjords and inlets where the silhouettes of glaciers are reflected back from the warm ocean. Ravens, which unlike crows never *caw*, call out from the deep forest with the croaks and rough whispers of their trickster tongue. Cormorants hold their cruciform wings out to dry on pilings. Herons and black oystercatchers haunt the shore, treading the still waters at low tide.

More than a hundred lives have been lost in shipwrecks here. Boats have been pulled down by whirlpools. (A contemporary nautical guide to the area offers advice on how to deal with this contingency: don't fight it, maintain your speed and steerage, use your momentum to ease out toward the edge.) The government tidal chart for the Yuculta rapids, an area renowned for strong and complex tidal currents, offers a separate current map for every hour in the day. A few miles west of those rapids, shamans thousands of years ago carved somber faces into twenty-six granite boulders on the shore, more than at any other site on the Pacific coast. The carvers are long gone, vanished but for these stone traces of mystery.

We would come in to Teakerne Arm with the *Cookie Monster* securely in tow, round the point, and catch sight of the lively waterfall with its cascade that was like the glistening, silvered flank of some great fish bursting from the ocean. There were often log booms arranged along either side of the inlet that offered secure and convenient moorage. My brothers and I would rush off to the waterfall, just like the English and Spanish explorers must have done almost two hundred years before us. We'd climb the narrow trail that led up the side of the escarpment and behind to Cassel Lake, a wide expanse of blue ringed by the dark forest. Somewhere in the boxes of photographs stowed away since my mother's death there is a snapshot of Bob and me standing on a little wharf at the edge of Cassel Lake with our fishing rods bent hard over the water as though a magnificent trout were thrashing at the end of each line. There were no fish on those rods:

we had deliberately hooked the lines beneath the dock. No fish, but great, wide smiles on our faces.

Meandering through these waters as a child, rowing to shore in this old dinghy, finding all the secret refuges of pleasure and mystery along the coast – those journeys were a joyful homecoming for me. In that territory, which so many have passed through and occupied but none have wholly owned, I made my own discoveries: simple moments of vibrancy and immediacy upon which I came to float as upon the wide and inviting sea.

With the buoyancy foam poured and the seats installed, the hull has undergone whatever small shifts in contour it will make. It's ready now for the keel and gunwales, the final defining structures of the boat. When this dinghy was first built there was no reliable means of attaching the keel except with fiberglass and fasteners. Now that I've filled all the old fastener holes and created a seamless, watertight hull, I don't intend to drill a bunch of new holes in it. Instead, I use epoxy as a structural mold. I abrade the hull along the length where the keel fits, abrade the matching surface of the keel, and glue the keel down. I then mix up a batch of epoxy thickened with tiny silica flakes; the curing heat of the amalgam begins to spread almost immediately. Using a mixing stick with the end rounded over, my gloved hands, a scrap of cardboard – whatever works – I create a fillet on either side of the keel where it joins the fiberglass. A fillet is a buttress, a coved profile of epoxy that solidly encases the joint. The resulting bond between keel and hull will be far stronger than fasteners, more watertight and almost infinitely durable.

I use a combination of steam bending and brute force to shape and place the maple gunwales along the curved hull. I glue them down with epoxy and then, realizing I have to give in to fasteners somewhere, I use small brass bolts to secure them to the hull, countersinking the bolts as I go so that the surfaces of the gunwales are smooth and continuous to the touch. I don't want any nasty surprises of metal on skin when I'm looking at the water ahead and feeling along the gunwale for a secure grip.

Last is the hardware. I retrieve the spars and sail from my dad's place among a substantial collection of sailing detritus: old spinnaker poles, rotting sails, a hurricane lamp. I'll replace all the lines and rigging – shackles, blocks, leads, halyards, stays, all of it – preserving only the oak mast step that my father made when the original one broke. It's reasonably well made. Sure, the mortise for the stub of the mast is slightly too large and the bearing surface where the step meets the hull is too rounded – but it's a serviceable, and meaningful, piece of hardware.

On my way home with the sail and rigging for *Cookie Monster* I pass the boatyard across from my dad's place. I'm reminded that most sailing vessels, small as dinghies or large as clipper ships, usually end their life on the rocks or in anonymous decay at a derelict wharfside. Captain Vancouver's *Discovery* served as a prison ship after its remarkable endeavor of exploration and was unceremoniously broken up at Deptford, on the Thames, in 1833. Today I see dozens of abandoned vessels at the boatyard, structures falling further into disrepair, stories falling toward the territory of the unremembered, freight of human experience slipping away with the tide. I suppose the reasonable thing is to think of memory and experience as residing not in boats (or cabinets or marimbas) but in the people who interact with them. But that's not how I see it. Somehow the memories reside in and are kept alive by the objects themselves. There is great resonance in things touched and shaped by hands. In whatever way you want to understand it, hokey or plain mysterious, objects made by caring hands are *alive*.

The last thing to go on the boat is its name. A local sign printer makes us a set of waterproof letters in clean, bright white:

Cookie Monster
Laird Family


The finished boat makes its way on a truck up to the lake. Elizabeth and I carefully unload it and carry it, like a child fresh from the womb, down to the water. Avery and Rowan scramble excitedly into their life jackets. The fresh and storied craft holds all four of us, the prescribed circumference of my world, neatly within its frame.

At the bow, water drips from Rowan's fingers as she withdraws them from the parted surface of the lake. A string of droplets splashes on the bright gunwale and traces a golden strand in the still air of morning. For a moment we are all quiet; there is only the swish of ripples across the hull. The oarlocks thrum in their new sockets, bronze fresh and burnished, as the oars twist them into the rhythm of service. A small wake eases out from the stern. The faces of my children, of my wife at the transom,

look out onto the lake as though each of them has mysteries to reveal.

Beyond the far trees, where an eagle perches atop a twisted cottonwood, the lightening sky spreads its radiance, touches the quiet waters and bursts into sinuous, dazzling shapes. The boat is steady with motion, pressing across the water, heading out from the gravel shore and the shadow of our little cabin. Farther out, the sun makes the lake glow as if with fire.

As I draw on the oars, easing the craft out into the bay, something in me unfurls toward what the day will bring: a gentle breeze, the sounds of children swimming, the rough-edged smoothness of a hull being pulled onto the beach. The warm air will wash the innocent day. The water, buoying us with its rhythms, will bear the weight of our memories and longings, our unremembered cargo of dreams.

## 7

# F I R E

LIGHT, AND FIRE. THIS IS HOW IT BEGINS, FAR
out on the horizon, beyond the threshold of shadows and
the deep well of the land's erasure. A vermilion hue like
the grain of purpleheart climbs into the eastern sky, slowly
transforms itself – to saffron, to coral, to the hue of steel
beneath a tempering flame – and comes to rest as a cerulean
expanse out of which the sun's great crest draws itself
upward into the lucent day. It is a moment of unen-
cumbered honesty, the sun so effortlessly, so implacably

threading its way into every hidden corner and labyrinthine refuge of shadow. To see what may be seen: into and through the solidity of my hands, the light penetrating and rendering them as kites of rice paper borne aloft; through the deep and patient weight of my bones, tissues folded inside like moths' wings with their hidden eyes.

By mid-morning the sun has stretched itself across the beam of our house and curled light round to the garden where strands of clematis meander along the fence above a bed of lantana and daylilies, the yellow and orange flowers like shards of flame. Above the shed a black squirrel perches head-down on the bark of an old cedar, clacking with dismissal as our cat Mowgli circles precisely on the grass below. At the rear of the yard a robust hydrangea marks the boundary beyond which a tangled forest slopes down toward the creek. The garden lantern I'm making will go here, between the hydrangea and a modest cedar shrub that reaches in sympathy back toward the trees.

Follow the trees far enough, down the canyon as it wends its way across the hillside toward the river and slopes into the bog with its acres of cranberry fields; just there, where the land levels itself out, you'll see the cedar mill perched at the river shore. The smell of fresh-cut wood drifts up to the traffic on the bridge above, and it's that smell, more than anything else, that tells me I'm home after a trip into the city: the scent of lemons roasted gently over a fire, of indigo flowers palm-crushed and

dried on bluffs over the desert. Cedar is the most aro-
matic of woods. Many others surrender their scents only
after patient inquiry – sometimes I stand quietly in my
shop with a stick of maple or beech or cherry held to my
nose, breathing in the subtle redolence of the wood
hidden deep in the pores. But cedar is exhibitionistic. I
can smell the mill from clear across the cranberry fields,
and if the wind is right, racing through the bog and up
the canyon behind our home, I've often thought I can
smell it from our backyard.

It's the fragrance of the wood, more than any other
biological factor, that accounts for the designation of
more than seventy species under the name of cedar. Only
the so-called true cedars – Lebanon, Atlas and deodar
(whose name means "god tree") – are members of the
genus *Cedrus*. The remaining species – eastern white,
Alaska, Port-Orford, western red and a host of others –
are unrelated to *Cedrus* and, generally, to each other. What
they all share is a rich and textured scent, excellent resis-
tance to decay, and a long heritage of association with
magic, insight, and illuminated clarity. The beams of the
temple of Solomon were made of cedar; totem poles are
carved of it; an ancient ceremonial ship buried in the
sands at Giza was planked with it. Like the trickster, cedar
mediates between worlds.[12]

It's warm inside the dry shed at the cedar mill. I stand
at the threshold, taking in the scents of the place: faint,

dry, and pervasive. Scents of every kind, from every place. It feels as though an army has marched across the globe and left the dust of its passing here, motes that hang in the air like luminous talismans buoyed by the sun. Many of those motes, released from the wood by the sawyer's hand, are aeons old, drifting in the air, inconsequential and annoying if I'm in a hurry. Yet if I slow down, they become gateways to astonishment, the way the smell of sea salt is a gateway to adventure. I smell honey and earth and rainy mornings as I pass the stacks near the entrance. Farther down, the aroma of dried fruit – figs, or perhaps apricots – drifts up from a ream of seasoned wood.

I amble over to a stack of western red and begin to choose pieces for the lantern legs. They range in color from salmon orange to almond brown, drawing these hues from differences between the lighter sapwood and the more dense heartwood. It's the heartwood pieces I'm particularly interested in, those with richly diverse grain and patterns of cross-grain figure that speckle the boards with rays and tiny, mottled flecks.

I select a dozen heartwood boards and check them for grain orientation, looking for pieces with internal growth rings that run roughly perpendicular to the surface of the board. Such quarter-sawn stock is more dimensionally stable, and more attractive, than flat-sawn wood cut with the growth rings parallel to the surface. I locate four candidates, tight-grained pieces dark enough to pass for walnut. The wood is smooth and soft, with fine undulations in the grain. It feels warm to the touch, a textured and resonant warmth.

The frames for the lantern glass will be made of yellow cedar, and there's quite a good collection of it here. It's more uniform in color than the red cedar but brighter, like candles glowing through amber. It doesn't take long to find several fine, clear pieces. I heft them onto my shoulder, pick up the red cedar boards (they're so *light*), pay the cashier and head for home, eager to start building my pillar of fire.

I have an image of what the lantern should look like but no measured drawing. It's a phantom I'm trying to coax into form. I sketch out a few ideas at the kitchen table, do a little research, begin playing with forms in the shop. I settle on a structure resembling a box kite with supports that curve down and outward to meet the ground and a shaped roof to keep out the rain. It's a simple design visually, but the actual construction joinery is more complex: there are bevels and splines and tight frames with interlocking grooves. I want to avoid traditional mortise-and-tenon joints, as my experience shaping them from cedar has been disappointing. Unlike maple or cherry, which can hold sharp and precise joint edges, cedar is quite soft and tends to crumble in the end grain of joints shaped by hand. Along the grain cedar is wonderfully clear and can be worked to a fine luster, which is one reason it is prized for carving. But in fine joinery it can be tricky, so instead of the traditional approach of mortise-and-tenon, I'll use biscuits instead. A woodworking biscuit is a small, flat wafer of beechwood in the shape of a football that's been stamped from a machine under tremendous pressure. When inserted with a little glue into crescent-shaped slots in the workpiece that match its contours – one slot on each face of the joint – the biscuit absorbs moisture from the glue and swells inside the joint, locking the pieces together. The resulting connection is quite strong. Still, biscuits are a newfangled invention and among traditionalists there has been a spirited debate about whether they provide as durable a solution as the mortise-and-tenon, intact examples of which date back to ancient Egypt. In the tests I've seen – a patient woodworker makes a bunch of mortise-and-tenon joints, a matched set of biscuited joints, and then breaks the whole works apart, measuring the force required for the joints to fail – biscuits do very well.

But there will always be, should always be, fierce debates in craft work about the hinge between the old and the new. That hinge should be rusty, squeaking in protest every time it's opened to usher change across the turbulent threshold. Walking that threshold entails the cultivation of a particular awareness – of frontiers and hidden passages. The Taoists called this deliberate cultivation "advancing the fire," or "planting lotuses in fire." For them, the manifest world is a fire that can both purify and consume. The lotus is individual awareness nurtured on that difficult ground. The Taoist orientation promotes a keen awareness of the edges where things meet; hanging out at the borders, watching the restless fringe for a glimpse of Wu Chi, the great primordial energy. One version of the oldest Taoist story, that of Fu Xi and his discovery of the eight trigrams, begins with Fu Xi sitting around a fire at night, out on the cold plain, studying the shifting pattern of flames above the wood. As the stacked logs burn, cracking into segments, they take the shapes of the trigram lines, one after the other, until Fu Xi sees all eight symbols in the fire. It's often this way: an awakening fire, far out on the frontier, offering an illuminated clarity of the true shape of things.

The only parts of this project I can't make myself are the glass panels, so I purchase them from a local glass artist and frame them in an afternoon. The biscuited joints go together tight and true. The sandblasted glass has a smoothed roughness that I find appealing, a translucence like contained fog, bright and clear, the way fog looks when the sun shines through it. And I notice, just now, that each yellow cedar frame − two long, vertical stiles enclosing two shorter rails − has the same number of segments and proportions as the trigram fire depicted at the beginning of this chapter. Two yangs enclose yin, the strength of cedar enclosing fluid and receptive glass. Or, as the *I Ching* says, "illumination with inner openness."

The Cherokee story of first days tells how humans were at one time ambivalent about illumination. They negotiated back and forth with Ouga, the creator, first desiring eternal sunlight and then, when it became unbearably hot, campaigning for constant night. Eventually the people asked Ouga to balance night and day, but not before many had died during the endless night with its hardships of cold and darkness. Ouga shaped a new tree in compassion and remembrance for the deceased, the *a-tsi-na tlu-gv,* or cedar, in which the departed spirits were invited to reside. The oldest cedars are thus ancestor trees; working with the wood of those trees is a sacrament, a communion of craftsmanship in which ancient bones step into the human world as witness to the centuries.

The curved lantern legs take shape on the bandsaw. I stand behind the blade, sighting down its length, holding the end of the workpiece in my left hand to guide it through. If the wood begins to meander from the line, I bring it back by swiveling my hand in the same direction – if it swings to the right of the line, I swivel it to the right. It's the same counterintuitive maneuvering as on a dinghy – if the boat swings downwind, point the tiller downwind. I position my right hand adjacent to the blade, nudging the wood slightly with my thumb and forefinger to maintain an accurate line of travel.

I try to follow the grain lines as much as possible, fitting the curved cuts on the saw to the natural direction of the wood's growth with its sweeps and turns always twisting toward the light. These are the palm lines of the tree – heart, head, sun, and fate – and like human palms, from which palmists take the meaning of breaks, branches, and forks, the grain lines of a tree illuminate its hidden life. In the work of craft, one must always search for that hidden life.

The aroma of cedar, first yellow and now red, infuses the shop. A natural fungicide in the wood makes that aroma and is the main reason why cedar is the wood of choice for outdoor projects. Fallen cedar logs in the forest will not rot away for centuries; properly cared for, cedar siding on a house can last 150 years. The longevity of the wood is astounding. The Egyptians, a culture singularly devoted to longevity in its many forms, often used cedar for the coffins inside sarcophagi. Working with it awakens me once again to the persistent and unfathomable spirit of craft. "The cedar does not decay," observed Origen almost two thousand years ago. "To use cedar for the beams of our house is to protect our soul from corruption."

At just over two feet in length, the lantern legs are a good stretch longer than any of the marimba keys, but since cedar is closely akin to redwood, I wonder if these legs might ring with their own sonorous notes. I locate the electronic tuner, now grimed with a carapace of sawdust after sitting idle so long, and whack one of the lantern legs with a marimba mallet. F-sharp, says the tuner. But what I hear is much more complex. A rich and sustained tone (the fundamental) is quickly followed by a deeper thrumming that seems to migrate slowly through the leg – I can see its vibration tracking back and forth across the surface. And I hear a third sound, more faint, that whispers out and is gone. Taken together, the sounds jostling and reaching and escaping, the notes make a rich music indeed. I begin to wonder about making another marimba, this time with larger keys, perhaps two or three feet long. How long would they have to be for me to hear the first and deepest sounds of the tree?

I cut biscuit slots on the inside faces of each leg to accept the panel frames. This requires careful measurement and alignment, which, as usual, I don't get quite right. It's one of those things, like spraying, that I don't ever expect to master. Funny thing: I can judge the thickness of a board to within a sixteenth of an inch by eye but can't seem to measure as accurately with a ruler. I've purchased a great many rulers over the years, instruments with all kinds of convenient innovations (including one involving the esoteric functions of the Fibonacci sequence) designed to make measuring easier and more precise. But these tools have not helped me a great deal, and I've made enough serious mistakes by way of faulty measuring – more than once ruining an entire project – that I now approach it with an obsessive dread. I will make the same measurement ten or fifteen times, straying to work on something else and coming back to it, rethinking my calculations, repeating my work with the ruler. And I experience the dread of knowing that my pickiness, my caution, my thoughtfulness will not always prevent me from cutting in the wrong place.

I try to avoid measuring if I can, choosing instead to size pieces against each other or in relation to story sticks, lengths of wood upon which I mark the dimensions of project parts – from this line to the end is the leg length, that mark there is where the biscuit goes. Story sticks with their myriad marks, penciled comments and pointing arrows are the totem poles of woodworking. And yet, despite my accurate story stick for the lantern, its marks precisely inscribed by careful measuring, I miscut two of the biscuit slots, one of which requires a repair that luckily, very luckily, will be covered by a panel frame.

An important illumination of my craft work has been that no matter how careful I am, things will go wrong. This insight in turn leads, if I watch closely enough, to one of the great secrets craft work reveals: I must accept my fate.

It helps to know first what that fate entails. Whether or not life will be messy, for example, glue spilling out of the joints as the clamps go together, hidden twists in the assemblies pulling everything out of true until I bang it all back into place, the insistence of my adjustments made more forceful by my knowledge that even now the biscuits are swelling in their tight spaces, almost granting me enough time to knock everything into its perfect place – straight and true – but setting up before I'm quite done. Fate is held and shaped by such moments, by the fire in them.

After gluing up the legs and panels, I apply two coats of finish. Of all the woodworking procedures and traditions, finishing gets the most attention in those fiery debates about old and new. It's usually the last stage in a project, the point where clouded and dusty surfaces are slowly transformed into fields of deep and textured illumination. This is a process of infusing the wood with light and fire, making clear what was once veiled, coaxing elusive shapes to emerge from a background of chiaroscuro. Modern finishes are chemical soups composed of materials like phenolic resins, ultraviolet light inhibitors, and foam reducers. The new, waterborne finishes in particular are impressively complex. The older, more traditional finishes are simpler: solvent, linseed oil, and varnish (with its own blend of plant-based or manufactured resins). On balance, the older finishes still provide the best way to achieve a lustrous finish. The difficulty with these finishes, and the reason waterborne finishes were developed, is that the solvents in traditional finish are volatile. When exposed to oxygen they can generate enough heat, especially in finish-soaked rags, to burst into flames. Traditional finishes are creatures of fire, seraphim, and if there is danger in them it is only the fire of illumination burning off the dross to reveal a lissome spirit within.[13]

The proportions of linseed oil, solvent, and varnish in traditional finish have been a matter of alchemical devotion in the history of woodworking even though the proportions don't really matter. The method of application varies slightly depending on how much varnish is in the mixture, but almost any combination of ingredients will do: more solvent, and the oil penetrates easily but builds up slowly; more varnish, and it builds up quickly but doesn't penetrate as well. Varnish and solvent may be removed from the mixture entirely, leaving only linseed or tung oil that imparts a clear, if not very protective, glow.[14]

Because the volatility of a traditional finish derives from the proportion of solvent in the mixture, reducing that volatility is simply a matter of adding more oil – typically linseed oil, which is also known as flaxseed oil and is sold under that name in my local health food store as a veritable panacea for modern ills. In Chinese medicine flax oil is sometimes used as a remedy for ailments generated by "excess fire" in the body.

The blend of ingredients I'm using here imparts to the finish a light and penetrating quality. The relatively high proportion of mineral spirits (the seraphim) helps deliver the oil into the wood pores. Most woodworkers choose a heftier proportion of varnish for outdoor projects, refinishing the piece every few years as the film wears down. I prefer to dress up the wood as little as possible, give it enough finish to highlight the grain but not so much that a barrier grows between the wood and its environment. After all, I'm delivering this wood back to the threshold of the forest, back to the frontier where the worked soil of our yard meets the tangled forest. The lantern will be a flame joining two worlds, and as the finish wears away, the cedar will begin to turn silver, over many long years molting into a silver exactly the color of ash from a hot fire.

I shape and join two wide boards to make the lantern's roof, beveling the edges so rain will run off, fashioning the joint between the roof and legs with unglued dowel pins to make the roof removable, noticing as I work that streaks of yellow and russet have begun to appear in the trees outside. Fall rain brings the season's first chill.

I apply one final coat of finish to the roof, secure the glass platform for the lighting source, and settle into the project's concluding steps. The rhythm slows. Avery helps me collect the many small offcuts that litter the shop floor, pieces too small for any useful woodworking purpose but which we use to build the first fire of the season. The wood burns hot and fast, the crackle of the flames lighting my son's face with a glow that seems also to come from within, as though the fire's ancient warmth calls forth his own hidden light.

During the week before Halloween I purchase a small gas lamp, the kind used for camping. I remove the lantern top and place the lamp on the glass platform inside. I take the lantern out to the back of the yard where summer trees are now shot through with amber and orange and a yellow bright as ripe papayas. The air is warm, though with a crisp undercurrent. The scent of fir and of damp soil, of dark and secret beginnings, drifts from the forest. In the week to come all the lights will be lit against the face of oncoming dark, jack-o'-lanterns and the spirit of

ritual illuminating the bright threads of connection between our diversities. The nourishing fires of community will come to life and string themselves across the landscape, individual watchfires in the shadow of long winter.

In anticipation of these changes, of the turning, of the sustenance and illumination of fire, I light the lantern.

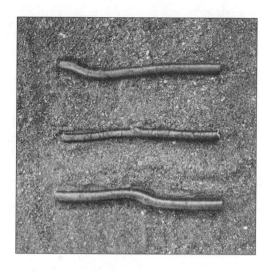

## 8

# THE UNFATHOMABLE

THE IDEA OF MAKING A MASK – OR A SERIES OF
masks, if all goes well – came about as the result of a
weekend trip that Elizabeth and I took to Tofino, on
Vancouver Island's west coast. It's a rugged, pristine area,
out on the threshold between far-flung land and endless
water, infused with a long history of cultural complexity.
We spent time in the town's galleries and craft shops, all of
which displayed masks and totems carved in the tradition
of aboriginal artists. There were stylized and elaborate

mythological motifs, emblazoned clan crests, ancient faces shaped by vanished hands. Tools passed down through numberless generations had worked the oldest pieces by firelight. Spirit voices spoke through precise mouths ringed with polished grain. I glimpsed ancestors, shapes of the invisible, smoke.

Prior to European contact, the cultures of the northwest coast embodied a highly developed consciousness of the heart. Dance and dream and the rhythm of time were threads of continuous, shining connection. Such an orientation inveighs against tinkering with a world of manifest sacredness, and as a result the complex technology required for the refinement of iron – to make hunting or carving tools – tends not to develop. When there is no scission from the source, from nature – when still we abide in the primordial garden – agriculture and metallurgy are less pressing aims. It is only when we leave the garden that technology flourishes.

Most peoples of the old world did not possess the technology to smelt iron or to harden it by heat treatment. Yet iron was known to them, and was sought out as a sacred metal particularly for the carving of ritual objects. In the far north, the Inuit made pilgrimages to Greenland, where, ten thousand years ago, meteoric iron fragments from the Cape York meteor impact spread out across the snow like dark splashes of ink on a pristine page. The Cape York debris is all that remains of a small planet that exploded in the formative stages of the solar system. Its iron is more than four billion years old – as old as the sun.

The Inuit used basalt, a hard volcanic stone, to chip off shards of the meteor, scrape them smooth and sharpen them. The resulting blades display the distinctive pattern of iron and nickel fused by galactic forces: they reflect light more softly, and in a wider spectrum, than does forged iron. It is the shimmering light of the most remote ago.

The location of the three largest Cape York meteor fragments – nicknamed The Woman, The Dog, and The Tent (Ahnighito) by the Inuit – was kept secret for millennia, known only to shamans. Then, in 1894, the site was hesitantly shown to Robert Peary, the Arctic explorer, who subsequently retrieved all three fragments – almost forty tons, with Ahnighito the size of a station wagon – and transported them to New York. They now reside in the Museum of Natural History (Ahnighito is supported by pillars that run through two floors of the museum and into the bedrock beneath the building). In the absence of a direct source of iron, the Inuit began trading for it, and many ritual tools were subsequently crafted from modified weaponry.

Tools cannot be separated from that which is made: they are twined, like means and ends. The essential spirit of creative work – elegant or indolent or visionary – not only derives from the craftsman's touch but is a legacy of the tool's character. In the case of the most ancient ritual masks and totems that I encountered in Tofino, that legacy is unfathomable. It is a benefaction of the Other, a remarkable gift of the invisible source.

Wrought iron, as opposed to that granted as a meteoric gift of the sky, has been used by seafaring nations for thousands of years. Masts and rigging from ships lost in storms would occasionally drift into the waters surrounding Tofino and be reclaimed. Cleats, turnbuckles, deck plates, knives – all were reshaped into ritual tools. Some are still in use today by the oldest aboriginal craftsmen. The works of those craftsmen are gifts of return, of thankfulness for a world so replete with mystery.

A week after our trip to Tofino, I stand in the great hall of the Museum of Anthropology in Vancouver, head bent back, gazing up forty feet to where precise images have been carved into cedar totem poles by craftsmen whose art has been almost entirely erased by time. This museum possesses one of the finest collections of carved wood artifacts in the world, and I feel quite at home here. Near the bottom of a nearby pole, a smooth-shouldered wolf rests in the shadow of a killer whale. The eye of the whale is a shadowed well. This wood, these bones, trace the nature and purpose of a vast awareness, a living spirit in the grain, each knot and every growth ring a secret hieroglyph worked carefully into many layers of meaning. The echo of leaves is here, the resonance of damp fields half submerged in twilight, of dark soil and tales of night. And long, interwoven strands of time knitted together by wood and human hands. The wood has been coaxed into shape – whittled, chiseled, sculpted with broad, incising strokes – by tools of utmost antiquity, by weapons, by stones, by meteors, by fragments of ships: countless forms oiled by luminous skin.

Although the focus of the collections is northwestern – hundreds of examples   I also find works from Indonesia and Greenland and China, specimens of all kinds and of diverse ages: an eagle with a five-foot, intricately carved beak, a tenebrous skull shape, moons and ravens and wild spirits of the forest. There are objects of great power here, and I am daunted by the virtuosity of craftsmanship displayed in so many of them. Working toward this level of refinement in carving will take me to the edge of my skill. But the spirit of creative work calls to whomever will listen, and as I gaze at these ethereal faces staring back from a lost age, their muted colors hiding a secret flame, once again I hear that whisper spiraling out from the primordial source of things.

In the instant I reach my hand to the wood and sense a silent energy thrumming inside, I become aware that many things will intrude to push and prod me out of this elemental state – mishaps and details and a pervasive lack of courage to do my absolutely best work – but an equal number will draw me back to the lucent and creative source. The stillness of that source lies behind the dream of an ancient, verdant grove that wakes me in the night, momentarily; it is the reason for my sudden pause, as I put the key in the lock, my knowledge that something fleetingly caught my eye – a shape I almost recognize – before stumbling into the house. Birds before morning and sand buried deep in the cold desert will together speak, reminding me that despite my umbrage and anticipation and indifference, behind my uncertain footfalls in the night's shadow, quiet, undeniable hands usher me onward.

Dark sky, cold rain, and a ground made bright by the sinuous shapes of wood sawn fresh from the tree: ivory of birch, faded porcelain of maple, linen of alder. There is some cypress, too, its scent of lemons reaching up from the wet soil to sting me with exhilaration. A black, rough flitch of walnut rests alongside the opened bole of a Douglas fir, its orange grain glowing from a sunrise heart. A woodpecker knocks once on the trunk of a cedar, then falls silent. I reach down to touch the alder, and in the moment of reaching, of touching the silent wood with its living core of mystery, it becomes clear what I must next do.

I've come again to Karl's ramshackle wood yard to find some pieces for carving. Nothing is clear yet, nothing except this first step, which is to make peace with the fallen, restless wood so newly taken from the forest: to retrieve it and begin the long process of drying slabs for carving. I've returned, as I so often do, to a careful beginning, these first few crucial steps in which I try to coax the wood into new life by listening and feeling for the prevailing needs of the old. This cannot be done lightly or casually; trees thwarted from their nature by ill use will inevitably turn on the craftsman, splitting and checking. The character of the work is revealed in these first moments.

Wind flaps the corner of a tarp. A small branch clatters to the ground. I choose four round alder sections, bark intact, checks not yet formed in the core. And I take the cypress, too, sawn into rough boards but still thick enough for carving work. The wood is heavy and wet. I hoist the pieces through the tailgate of my station wagon and head home, listening for that discourse I know will come; the gentle opening of suggestions and demands and imprecations through which the work will slowly begin to grow. It is always thus, listening and waiting and reaching for an inscrutable source that guides my hand as a valley guides the river, shaping and being shaped as it wends toward the sea.

On top of the stack of Douglas fir beside my house a niche has been left by the boards I used to make the keel and seats for the dinghy. I place the alder and cypress in this niche. The wood lies neatly cocooned, taken in by the fir like a guest from the rain. It will rest here, somnolent through winter and fragrant in summer, until I can bring it into the shop for final drying.

As I cover the stack, my thoughts turning to the work ahead, I acknowledge that the wood's redemption — its escape from dissolution — is also my own. We are bound now, fragments of becoming. We share the journey of the totem; the faces of the figures are hidden in my hand.

The totem is a spiritual heraldry. It describes, through a vast shorthand, the indications of the unfathomable. It is a finger pointing to the beginning, a wind blowing from a pristine field of possibility. It relates the tale of meteoric iron birthed as companion to the sun. Totems, like tools and the quiet in my shop, are reminders to remember, and to act.

I step into the landscape of my own totem. I see my grandmother, the falcon, her brow etched like the grain of rough cedar, weathered by war, made bright with family. I hear the voice of my mother, the wolf: first a clear call, then a tremor, and finally a wail. I feel the hands of my father, the porpoise: bashed thumb, strong fingers, palm enough like my own that I sometimes watch, looking for myself.

The territory brightens with faces. I find the eagle, Elizabeth, she who carries and sustains, whose touch is redolent with solace. Rowan, the deer, blackberry stains

on her chin, shouts with joy as she runs through the golden field. And Avery, the seal, cradled by wonder, darts into the light.

In my own hands I study the small whittling scars, the insignia left by a mishap with bleached coral, the numb place where I almost sliced off my finger cutting firewood in the rain. I wonder what indelible traces will be left by this next endeavor — teeth marks from carved mouths. I reach toward a horizon of prophecy, to mentors and unknown guides, to an unbroken cord of lineage secured at the source by invisible hands.

This is where I begin: with everything.

# NOTES

1. Frank Wilson, *The Hand: How Its Use Shapes the Brain, Language and Human Culture* (New York: Vintage, 1998). Wilson demonstrates convincingly that "delicate and precise motor control is a potential capability of the entire upper limb (140)." This is a counterintuitive conclusion, especially to beginning carvers and artists whose tendency is to rely on the internal muscles of the thumb and fingers to control delicate, incisive movements. With practice, though, it becomes clear that using the entire arm not only is a more effective strategy in terms of strength (which is useful in carving) but also makes possible precise, sweeping movements that the thumb and fingers alone are quite limited in producing.

2. Liu I-ming, *The Taoist I Ching,* trans. Thomas Cleary (Boston: Shambhala, 1986), 210. Throughout the text I have used Cleary's excellent translation of Liu I-ming's 1796 distillation of essential Taoist teaching. There are many versions of the *I Ching,* some of which are virtually impenetrable to Western readers with little knowledge of Chinese philosophy. Cleary's various translations and compilations are refreshing; they open a window into the ancient culture and spirituality of China in a most accessible way.

3. A cutaway of the oldest authentically dated tree in the world – a bristlecone pine from the White Mountains in eastern California – is on display at the American Museum of Natural History in New York City. It's roughly 4,500 years old, and began growing at the time the Egyptians built the pyramids.

4. Bart Hopkin, *Musical Instrument Design* (Tuscon: See Sharp Press, 1996), 34.

5. David Welter recommends this angle in his article "Wooden Planes," *Fine Woodworking,* October 1997, 69.

6. Sun Tzu, *The Art of War,* trans. Thomas Cleary (Boston: Shambhala, 1988), 16. Sun Tzu's *Art of War* is among the great Taoist classics that have come down to us from remote antiquity (the others are the *I Ching* and the *Tao Te Ching*). There are references in the most ancient literature to earlier books: the *Lien Shan,* "Mountains Standing Together" and *Kuei Ts'ang,* "Reverting to the

Hidden." These latter books have been lost for over two millennia, but originally made up, along with the *I Ching,* the original canon of Taoist thought. The *I Ching,* one of the richest and most complex books of wisdom in the world, is thus only a fragment of a much larger sacred literature now completely vanished, "cloud-hidden, whereabouts unknown."

7. There is also some evidence that ancient Chinese explorers traveled as far east as North America in search of jade and the sacred mushrooms (or fungus) of immortality. Moreover, visitors from the far west figure prominently in northwestern myth and legend, as do tales of an ancient, true homeland in the west that was destroyed by flood and fire.

8. Lewis Hyde, *Trickster Makes This World: Mischief, Myth and Art* (New York: North Point Press, 1998), 258.

9. The world's tallest tree (though not the largest; the General Sherman tree, at 2,200 tons, is the most massive) is currently the Mendocino tree, a coast redwood, near Ukiah, California, at 367½ feet. One of its neighbors was slightly higher until a winter storm broke ten feet off its top. Taller and larger trees than these have been documented: one of them, a Douglas fir in Mission, British Columbia – about forty miles from my home – measured 415 feet. Legends, of course, speak of trees that were higher still. In the ancient epic of Gilgamesh, the trees of the sacred cedar forest reach all the way to heaven.

10. Samuel Bawlf has made a compelling argument that Vancouver, Valdes and Galiano were not the first Europeans to explore the Inside Passage. Bawlf asserts that Francis Drake, on a clandestine mission for Elizabeth I, navigated through the Inside Passage and made it as far north as Alaska nearly two centuries earlier.

11. Menzies was the first European to study the Douglas fir, the Latin name of which, *Pseudotsuga menziesii,* bears his name.

12. One legend holds that Solomon cut down a Lebanon cedar and buried it where the pool of Bethesda later came to be. A thousand years later, the tree floated to the surface of the pool before Christ's crucifixion and was used as the upright of the cross.

13. The central aims of medieval alchemy were the transmutation of base metals into gold — as a metaphor for spiritual refinement — finding the elixir of life and discovering the "universal solvent" (which, by the way, turns out to be water). Every contemporary woodworker during the finishing stages of a project is a modern alchemist.

14. I am indebted to Garrett Hack and Chris Minick for their finishing advice in the pages of *Fine Woodworking* magazine. Hack's mixture (equal parts linseed oil, spar varnish and turpentine) yields a tough, durable sheen with a distinctive, hand-rubbed look ("Oil-Varnish Mixture Is Durable, Easy to Apply," February 1997, 48).

Minick's version (1½ cups mineral spirits, 1 cup brushing varnish, ¼ cup linseed oil) penetrates exceptionally well and prevents oil bubbling on ring-porous woods like oak (Finish Line, October 1999, 129).

The text in this book is set in Bembo, a typeface produced by Stanley Morison of Monotype in 1929. Bembo is based on a roman typeface cut by Francesco Griffo in 1495; the companion italic is based on a font designed by Giovanni Tagliente in the 1520s.

The display is set in Weiss, a typeface designed by Rudolf Weiss in 1926 and based on typefaces from the Italian Renaissance.

Book design by Ingrid Paulson

Photographs by Elizabeth A. Laird

Line drawings by Bill Slavin